Careers in Focus

CHILD CARE

Careers in Focus

CHILD CARE

Ferguson
An imprint of Infobase Publishing

Ferguson
An imprint of Infobase Publishing
132 West 31st Street
New York NY 10001

Library of Congress Cataloging-in-Publication Data

Careers in focus. Child care.
    p. cm.
  Includes index.
  ISBN 0-8160-6565-9 (hc : alk. paper)
  1. Child care—Vocational guidance—Juvenile literature. I. J. G. Ferguson Publishing Company. II. Title: Child care.
  HQ778.5.C369 2007
  649.023'73—dc22   2006009220

Ferguson books are available at special discounts when purchased in bulk quantities for businesses, associations, institutions, or sales promotions. Please call our Special Sales Department in New York at (212) 967-8800 or (800) 322-8755.

You can find Ferguson on the World Wide Web at http://www.fergpubco.com

Text design by David Strelecky

Printed in the United States of America

MP Hermitage 10 9 8 7 6 5 4 3 2 1

This book is printed on acid-free paper.

Table of Contents

Introduction

Careers in Focus: Child Care describes a variety of careers in the rewarding world of child care—in child care centers, hospitals, medical offices, libraries, schools, and countless other settings. These careers are as diverse in nature as they are in their earnings and educational requirements.

A few of these careers—such as nannies, child care workers, and teacher aides—require little formal education, but are excellent starting points for a career in the industry. Others—such as child care service owners, coaches, neonatal nurses, preschool teachers, and school nurses—require some postsecondary training. The majority of careers in the child care and services industry, though, require a bachelor's degree (such as child life specialists, elementary school teachers, social workers, and special education teachers) or a master's degree (such as child psychologists, children's librarians, creative arts therapists, guidance counselors, and speech-language pathologists and audiologists). The career of pediatrician requires a medical degree. Earnings range from less than $12,000 for beginning nannies and child care workers to more than $200,000 for experienced pediatricians.

The employment outlook for the child care industry is excellent. Workers in various disciplines will always be needed to care for the physical, social, mental, and educational needs of children. Especially strong career opportunities will be available for child care service owners, child psychologists, neonatal nurses, social workers, special education teachers, speech-language pathologists and audiologists, and teacher aides. In addition, child care workers and nannies will enjoy good employment prospects, as these careers feature a large number of available positions. In fact, the U.S. Department of Labor predicts that employment in the child daycare services industry will grow by 43 percent through 2012.

Each article in this book discusses a particular child care and services occupation in detail. The articles in *Careers in Focus: Child Care & Services* appear in Ferguson's *Encyclopedia of Careers and Vocational Guidance,* but have been updated and revised with the latest information from the U.S. Department of Labor, professional organizations, and other sources. The following paragraphs detail the sections and features that appear in the book.

The **Quick Facts** section provides a brief summary of the career, including recommended school subjects, personal skills, work environment, minimum educational requirements, salary ranges, certification or licensing requirements, and employment outlook. This section also provides acronyms and identification numbers for the following government classification indexes: the *Dictionary of Occupational Titles* (DOT), the *Guide for Occupational Exploration* (GOE), the National Occupational Classification (NOC) index, and the Occupational Information Network (O*NET)-Standard Occupational Classification System (SOC) index. The DOT, GOE, and O*NET-SOC indexes have been created by the U.S. government; the NOC index is Canada's career classification system. Readers can use the identification numbers listed in the Quick Facts section to access further information about a career. Print editions of the DOT (*Dictionary of Occupational Titles*. Indianapolis, Ind.: JIST Works, 1991) and GOE (*The Guide for Occupational Exploration*. 3d ed. Indianapolis, Ind.: JIST Works, 1993) are available at libraries. Electronic versions of the NOC (http://www23.hrdc-drhc. gc.ca) and O*NET-SOC (http://online.onetcenter.org) are available on the World Wide Web. When no DOT, GOE, NOC, or O*NET-SOC numbers are present, this means that the U.S. Department of Labor or Human Resources Development Canada have not created a numerical designation for this career. In this instance, you will see the acronym "N/A," or not available.

The **Overview** section is a brief introductory description of the duties and responsibilities involved in this career. Often, a career may have a variety of job titles. When this is the case, alternative career titles are presented.

The **History** section describes the history of the particular job as it relates to the overall development of its industry or field.

The **Job** describes the primary and secondary duties of the job.

Requirements discusses high school and postsecondary education and training requirements, any certification or licensing that is necessary, and other personal requirements for success in the job.

Exploring offers suggestions on how to gain experience in or knowledge of the particular job before making a firm educational and financial commitment. The focus is on what can be done while still in high school (or in the early years of college) to gain a better understanding of the job.

The **Employers** section gives an overview of typical places of employment for the job.

Starting Out discusses the best ways to land that first job, be it through the college placement office, newspaper ads, or personal contact.

The **Advancement** section describes what kind of career path to expect from the job and how to get there.

Earnings lists salary ranges and describes the typical fringe benefits.

The **Work Environment** section describes the typical surroundings and conditions of employment—whether indoors or outdoors, noisy or quiet, social or independent. Also discussed are typical hours worked, any seasonal fluctuations, and the stresses and strains of the job.

The **Outlook** section summarizes the job in terms of the general economy and industry projections. For the most part, Outlook information is obtained from the U.S. Bureau of Labor Statistics and is supplemented by information taken from professional associations. Job growth terms follow those used in the *Occupational Outlook Handbook*. Growth described as "much faster than the average" means an increase of 36 percent or more. Growth described as "faster than the average" means an increase of 21 to 35 percent. Growth described as "about as fast as the average" means an increase of 10 to 20 percent. Growth described as "more slowly than the average" means an increase of 3 to 9 percent. Growth described as "little or no change" means an increase of 0 to 2 percent. "Decline" means a decrease of 1 percent or more.

Each article ends with **For More Information,** which lists organizations that provide information on training, education, internships, scholarships, and job placement.

Careers in Focus: Child Care also includes photos, informative sidebars, and interviews with professionals in the field.

Child Care Service Owners

QUICK FACTS

School Subjects
Business
Family and consumer science

Personal Skills
Helping/teaching
Leadership/management

Work Environment
Primarily indoors
Primarily one location

Minimum Education Level
Some postsecondary training

Salary Range
$17,680 to $26,100 to
$60,000

Certification or Licensing
Required by certain states

Outlook
Faster than the average

DOT
N/A

GOE
12.03.03

NOC
N/A

O*NET-SOC
39-9011.00

OVERVIEW

Child care service owners provide care for infants, toddlers, and preschool-aged children. While the parents and guardians are at work, child care providers watch the children and help them develop skills through games and activities. The child care service may be part of the owner's home, or it may be a separate center composed of classrooms, play areas, and areas for infant care. The service owner must hire, train, and schedule child care workers, or teachers, to assist with large numbers of children. The owner must also manage the center's finances, assure that the center meets legal requirements and accreditation standards, and meet with prospective clients. Child care centers are in demand all across the country, as the majority of parents of young children have jobs outside the home. There are approximately 456,000 child care workers in the United States. According to the National Child Care Association, there are more than 120,000 licensed child care centers in the United States.

HISTORY

Most people probably think daytime child care is a fairly modern idea. It's true that only 17 percent of the mothers of one-year-olds were part of the labor force in 1965. That number seems small when compared to statistics from the U.S. Department of Labor—today, approximately 65 percent of mothers of children under age six are working outside the home. But child care centers were needed as far back as the 18th century. In England, factories opened nurseries to care for the workers' children, a trend that carried over to the United States in the 19th century. Of course, working conditions in factories were often terrible before the 1900s, and the children were put to work at very young ages. So the child care service as we know it today didn't really begin to evolve until World War II, when women joined the workforce while the men were off fighting. Though many of these women quit their jobs when the men returned from the war, roles for women began to change. The last half of the 20th century saw more opportunities for women in the workplace and, for many families, two incomes became necessary to meet the rising costs of living. Findings by the U.S. Census Bureau indicate that today only about 15 percent of married couples with young children have one parent working and one parent staying at home. Some 65 percent of women with children under the age of six are in the labor force. This has generated a great demand for dependable, safe child care services.

THE JOB

Child care workers are responsible for taking care of several children of various ages every single workday, and owners of child care services must make sure that the care the children receive is of the highest possible quality. Parents expect those working at care centers to help their children learn basic skills, such as using a spoon and playing together, and to prepare them for their first years of school by, for example, teaching colors and letters. Service owners come up with activities that build on children's abilities and curiosity. Attending to the individual needs of each child is important, so that activities can be adapted to specific needs. For example, a three-year-old child has different motor skills and reasoning abilities than a child of five years of age, and the younger child will need more help completing the same project. Child care centers typically provide care for babies, toddlers, and children of pre-kindergarten age, and because of this, they offer many different kinds of instruction. Some kids will just be learning how to tie their shoes and button their coats, while others will have begun to develop reading and computer skills. And, of course, the infants require much individual attention for things such as feedings, diaper changings, and being held when awake. Owners of small facilities are typically the primary care givers and do the majority of these activities in addition to the administrative activities involved in running a business—ordering supplies, paying the bills, keeping records, making sure the center meets licensing requirements, and so forth. Owners of large facilities hire aides, teachers, and assistant directors to help provide care.

Nancy Moretti owns a child care center in Smithfield, Rhode Island, called Just For Kids. The center is licensed to care for 54 children and is composed of five classrooms—each room for a different age group. She has a staff of 18 who work with kids from six weeks to five years old. "Everyone here loves children," Moretti says. "We're an extended family; we all look out for each other." Moretti's day starts with a walk through the classrooms to make sure everything is in order and to make sure all the staff members and children are there. Much of Moretti's work consists of attending to staff concerns, such as payment and scheduling. When hiring teachers for her center, she looks for people with some background in child development, such as a college degree or some years of practical experience.

A background in child development gives owners and teachers the knowledge of how to create a flexible and age-appropriate schedule that allows time for music, art, playtime, academics, rest, and other activities. Owners and child care staff work with the youngest children to teach them the days of the week and to recognize colors, seasons, and animal names and characteristics; older children are taught number and letter recognition and simple writing skills. Self-confidence and the development of communications skills are encouraged in day care centers. For example, children may be given simple art projects, such as finger painting, and after the paintings are completed everyone takes a turn showing and explaining the finished projects to the rest of the class. Show and tell gives students opportunities to speak and listen to others. Other skills children are taught may include picking up their toys after play time and washing their hands before snack time.

Owners of both small and large facilities have many other responsibilities aside from lessons and instruction. They may need to spend a large portion of a day comforting a child, helping him or her to adjust to being away from home, and finding ways to include the child in group activities. Children who become frightened or homesick need reassurance. Children also need help with tasks, such as putting on and taking off their coats and boots in the winter. If a child becomes sick, the owner must decide how to handle the situation and may contact the child's parents, a doctor, or even a hospital. Owners also order supplies for activities and supervise events, such as snack time, during which they teach children how to eat properly and clean up after themselves.

Child care center owners also work with the parents of each child. It is not unusual for parents to come to preschool and observe a child or go on a field trip with the class, and child care workers often take these opportunities to discuss the progress of each child as well as any specific problems or concerns. Scheduled meetings are available for parents who cannot visit the school during the day. Moretti makes it a point to be frequently available for the parents when they're dropping off and picking up the children. "Parents need to know that I'm here," she says. "For the owner to be involved is important to the parents."

REQUIREMENTS

High School
You should take courses in early childhood development when available. Many home economics courses include units in parenting and child care. English courses will help you to develop communication skills important in dealing with children, their parents, and a child care staff. In teaching children, you should be able to draw from a wide base of education and interests, so take courses in art, music, science, and physical education. Math and accounting courses will prepare you for the bookkeeping and management requirements of running your own business.

Postsecondary Training
A college degree isn't required for you to open a day care center, but it can serve you in a variety of ways. A child development program will give you the background needed for classroom instruction, as well as for understanding the basics of child care and psychology. A college degree will also demonstrate to your clients that you have the background necessary for good child care. A college degree program should include course work in a variety of liberal arts subjects, including English, history, and science, as well as nutrition, child development, psychology of the young child, and sociology.

Certification or Licensing
Requirements for the licensing or registering of child care workers vary from state to state. You can visit the website of the National Child Care Information Center (http://nccic.org), part of the Administration for Children and Families, to find out about your state's regulatory bodies and contact information. Requirements for a child care administrator, director, or owner may include having a certain amount of child care experience or education, completing a certain amount of continuing education per year, being at least 21 years of age, and having a high school diploma. Cardiopulmonary resuscitation training is also often required. National certification may not be required of child care service owners and workers in every state, but some organiza-

tions do offer it. The Council for Professional Recognition offers the Child Development Associate (CDA) National Credentialing Program. To become a CDA, you must meet competency standards and have experience in child care. There are more than 150,000 CDAs across the country. The National Child Care Association offers the National Administrator Credential (NAC). To receive this credential, you must complete a special five-day training course. (Contact information for these organizations is at the end of this article.)

Other Requirements

Obviously, a love for children and a concern for their care and safety are most important in this line of work. Child care comes naturally to most of those who run child care services. "I can't see myself doing anything but this," Nancy Moretti says. You should be very patient and capable of teaching children in many different stages of development. Because young children look up to adults and learn through example, it is important that a child care worker be a good role model—you should treat the children with respect and kindness, while also maintaining order and control. You must also be good at communicating with the parents, capable of addressing their concerns, and keeping them informed as to their children's progress.

EXPLORING

You can gain experience in this field by volunteering at a child care center or other preschool facility. Some high schools provide internships with local preschools for students interested in working as teacher's aides. Your guidance counselor can provide information on these opportunities. Summer day camps or Bible schools with preschool classes also hire high school students as counselors or counselors-in-training. Take tours of child care centers of various sizes, and talk to the owners about how they started their businesses.

EMPLOYERS

According to data from the National Child Care Association, there are more than 120,000 licensed child care centers in the United States. Child care centers are located all across the country. Those who buy an established day care facility often find that most of the clients will come along with it. For those who start their own centers, word-of-mouth, a variety of offerings, and a good reputation will draw clients. Franchising is a viable option in this industry. Child care franchising operations are among the fastest growing centers.

Primrose School Franchising Company and Kids 'R' Kids International are two of the child care companies offering franchises.

In some cases, people work from their homes, watching only their own children and some of the children from their neighborhoods; this is usually referred to as "family child care."

STARTING OUT

At your first opportunity, you should take part-time work at a child care center to gain firsthand experience. Contact child care centers, nursery schools, Head Start programs, and other preschool facilities to learn about job opportunities. Often there are many jobs for child care workers listed in the classified sections of newspapers. The turnover rate for child care workers is high because of the low wages and long hours. "You need to make sure child care is something you want to do," Nancy Moretti says, "before starting your own center." Some owners of child care centers are not actively involved with the day-to-day running of the business; parents, however, prefer to leave their children at a center where the owner takes an active interest in each child's well-being. Moretti purchased a day care center that had been in operation for nearly 10 years, and she had worked as a teacher and director at that center for eight of them. Knowing all the parents already helped her ease into ownership without losing a single client. For those considering buying an established daycare center, Moretti recommends that they spend a few months getting to know the parents first.

ADVANCEMENT

As an owner's child care center becomes better known in the community, and as it gains a reputation for providing quality child care, owners may advance by expanding their businesses. With enough income, owners can hire staff members to help with child care, instruction, and administrative requirements. Nancy Moretti is currently in the process of expanding Just For Kids in a variety of ways. She'll be putting an addition onto the building to allow for a number of new services: a full-day kindergarten, a before- and after-school program, and a summer day camp. Moretti also recently sent surveys out to the parents to determine whether Saturday child care is needed.

In addition to expanding offerings at one child care center, some owners choose to open more centers. Primrose School Franchising Company, for example, notes that 30 percent of its franchisees own two or more Primrose Schools.

EARNINGS

It is difficult to determine exact salaries for child care service owners since revenue for child care centers varies according to the number of children cared for, whether the center is owned or rented, number of staff, and other factors. A center in a city with a higher cost of living and more staffing and licensing requirements will charge more than a center in a smaller town. No matter where it is located, however, a large percentage of a child care center's earnings goes to paying the staff. In 2001, Americans spent $31 billion on licensed child care. A 2005 report by the Children's Defense Fund found that parents paid an annual average of between $4,000 and $10,000 nationwide for the care of a four-year-old at a child care center. If a center cared for 54 children (like Nancy Moretti's) and charged $4,000 per child, the center's annual budget would be $216,000. Although this sounds like a fair amount of money, keep in mind that staff salaries must come out of this amount, and these usually account for 60 percent to 70 percent of expenses. Sixty percent of $216,000 is $129,600, which leaves the owner with $86,400 to pay for all other expenses, such as any rent or mortgage on the center, any maintenance expenses, any food served, liability insurance premiums, and other equipment or items that are needed, such as playground equipment, paper cups, or books. After all such expenses are paid, owners can then draw their salaries.

According to the Center for the Child Care Workforce, center directors had hourly earnings that ranged from $8.50 to $24.79 in 2001. Someone working at this rate for 40 hours a week year-round would earn $17,680 to $51,563 annually. The U.S. Department of Labor reports the median earnings for all child care workers were $8.68 per hour in 2004. Someone working at this rate for 40 hours a week year-round would have an annual income of approximately $16,950. The department also reports the lowest paid 10 percent of child care workers earned less than $5.93 per hour (approximately $12,330 annually), and the highest paid 10 percent earned more than $12.55 per hour (approximately $26,100 annually). A child care center owner just starting out in the business and working as the only employee may have earnings comparable to that of the average child care worker. An experienced child care service owner running a large and well-established center, on the other hand, may have annual earnings in the $60,000s.

Since they run their own businesses, owners must pay for their own benefits, such as health insurance and retirement plans.

WORK ENVIRONMENT

Center owners spend a lot of time on their feet, helping staff, directing children, and checking on classrooms. Most child care centers have play areas both inside and outside. In the spring and summer months, owners—especially those with a small staff or none at all—may spend some time outside with the kids, leading them in playground exercises and games. The colder winter months will keep the kids confined mostly indoors. Though child care workers can control the noise somewhat, the work conditions are rarely quiet. An owner's work is divided between child care and administrative responsibilities, but the size of the center often determines how much time is spent on each. For example, the owner of a small service with one part-time employee will spend most of the day with the children, directing activities, serving snacks, settling arguments over toys, and talking with parents as they drop off or pick up their children. For the most part, this owner will do administrative work—record keeping of attendance, billing for services, paying the center's bills, filing tax forms—during short periods of free time in the day and during the evenings and on weekends when the center is closed. Owners of large centers with several staff members often have more time during the day to attend to administrative duties. Even these owners, however, often work on business matters after hours. Nancy Moretti's center is open Monday through Friday, 6:30 A.M. to 6:00 P.M., but she also works weekends. "It's fun most of the time," she says, despite 70 to 80 hour workweeks.

OUTLOOK

The U.S. Department of Labor projects overall employment in the field of child care services to grow faster than the average through 2012. More women than ever are part of the workforce; of those who have children, many take only an abbreviated maternity leave. The Children's Defense Fund reports that every day more than 12 million preschool-aged children in the United States are in some type of child care. By 2010, the nation will have another 1.2 million children aged four and under. Corporations have tried to open their own day care centers for the children of employees but haven't always had much success. Often these corporations turn to outside sources and contract with independent care centers to meet these child care needs.

Staffing problems in general plague the child care industry, as centers struggle to find reliable, long-term employees. Other concerns of child care centers include providing better child care for low-income families; making child care more inclusive for children with disabilities; and possible competition from state funded pre-kindergarten programs.

On the bright side, though, licensed child care centers continue to open and provide opportunities for those wanting to run their own businesses. Those centers that offer a number of services, such as after-school programs for older children and computer instruction for children at a variety of age levels, should have the most success and continue to draw new clients.

FOR MORE INFORMATION

For information about the CDA credential, contact
Council for Professional Recognition
2460 16th Street, NW
Washington, DC 20009-3575
Tel: 800-424-4310
http://www.cdacouncil.org

Visit the NAEYC website to read relevant articles concerning issues of child care and to learn about membership and accreditation for programs.
National Association for the Education of Young Children (NAEYC)
1509 16th Street, NW
Washington, DC 20036
Tel: 800-424-2460
http://www.naeyc.org

For information about student memberships and training opportunities, contact
National Association of Child Care Professionals
PO Box 90723
Austin, TX 78709-0723
Tel: 800-537-1118
Email: admin@naccp.org
http://www.naccp.org

For information about the NAC credential and to learn about the issues affecting child care, visit the NCCA webpage or contact
National Child Care Association (NCCA)
2025 M Street, NW, Suite 800
Washington, DC 20036-3309
Tel: 202-367-1133
Email: info@nccanet.org
http://www.nccanet.org

INTERVIEW

Karen Ballard has worked in the child care field for 10 years. She is the regional director of The Learning Tree Child Care Center, which has three locations—two in Livonia, Michigan, and one in South Lyon, Michigan. Karen was kind enough to discuss her career with the editors of Careers in Focus: Child Care.

Q. Why did you decide to pursue a career in child care administration?

A. I decided to become an administrator because I wanted to make a difference in the lives of children and their families. I wanted to offer children a home away from home—somewhere where they could feel safe and loved, have fun just being a kid, and where they could learn and grow into their own unique selves in an environment where individuality and creativity is encouraged.

Q. What are your typical tasks/responsibilities as a regional director?

A. I oversee the directors who oversee the daily operation of each facility. With that, I write and implement new policies and procedures, train administration and teachers, act as parent liaison, oversee budgets and enrollment of each center, develop new and creative programs, and take part in hiring. When a new center is opened I am involved in the design process and do the arrangement and decorating. I also oversee marketing and advertising, and somehow still find time to do what I love best—play in the classroom with the children.

Q. What are the three most important professional qualities for child care service workers?

A. They need to be team players, have a high work ethic, and have passion!

Q. What advice would you give to high school students who are interested in this career?

A. Work hard—working with children is not easy but it is very rewarding. Make sure that working with children is your passion, and you will succeed. I would also say observe some child care centers to get a feel for what child care is all about before making a career decision. Talk to someone who has been in the field for a while.

Child Care Workers

QUICK FACTS

School Subjects
Art
Family and consumer science

Personal Skills
Communication/ideas
Helping/teaching

Work Environment
Primarily indoors
Primarily one location

Minimum Education Level
High school diploma

Salary Range
$12,330 to $16,950 to
$26,100

Certification or Licensing
Recommended (certification)
Required by certain states
(licensing)

Outlook
About as fast as the average

DOT
359

GOE
12.03.03

NOC
6474

O*NET-SOC
39-9011.00

OVERVIEW

Child care workers are employed by day care centers, preschools, and other child care facilities and work with infants, toddlers, and preschool-aged children. While parents and guardians are at work, child care providers watch the children and help them develop skills through games and activities. Today there are approximately 456,000 child care workers, outside of preschool teachers and teacher assistants, in the United States. According to the National Child Care Association, there are currently more than 120,000 licensed child care centers in the United States.

HISTORY

You probably think daytime child care is a fairly modern idea. It's true that only 17 percent of the mothers of one-year-olds were part of the labor force in 1965. That number seems small when you look at statistics from the U.S. Census Bureau—today, approximately 55 percent of mothers with infants (children under the age of one) are in the workforce. Additionally, most pre-school-aged children are cared for in child care centers, according to findings by the Center for Women in the Economy. But child care centers were needed as far back as the 18th century.

In England, factories employed child care workers to run nurseries for the factory workers' children, a trend that carried over to the United States in the 19th century. Of course, working conditions in factories were often terrible before the 1900s, and the children were put to work at very young ages. So the child care service as we know it today didn't really begin to evolve until World War II, when

Child care workers need a great deal of patience and the ability to understand the needs of children in all stages of development. *(Jim Whitmer Photography)*

women joined the workforce while the men were away fighting. Though many of these women quit their jobs when the men returned from the war, roles for women began to change. In the last half of the 20th century there were more opportunities for women in the workplace, and for many families, two incomes became necessary to meet the rising costs of living. Daytime child care consequently became necessary. The U.S. Census Bureau reports that by the end of the 20th century, in close to 70 percent of married couples with children under age 18, both the husband and wife held paying jobs. Since the bureau projects the number of children under 18 to increase from approximately 70 million in 1999 to about 77 million in 2020, dependable, safe, and caring child care services will continue to be in high demand.

THE JOB

Anyone who has ever baby-sat or worked with a group of kids in a summer camp knows something about the demands of child care. Professional child care workers take on the responsibility of providing quality care to young children. But the parents don't just expect these workers to simply keep an eye on the kids while they're at work—they also expect child care workers to help the children learn basic skills and to prepare them for their first years of school. Child care workers assist teachers and center directors in coming up with activities that build on children's abilities and curiosity. Child care workers must also pay attention to the individual needs of each child so that they can adapt activities to these specific needs. For example, a worker should plan activities based on the understanding that a three-year-old child has different motor skills and reasoning abilities than a child five years of age. Because child care workers care for babies, toddlers, and kids of pre-kindergarten age, these workers need to provide many different kinds of instruction. Some kids will just be learning how to tie their shoes and button their coats, while others will have begun to develop reading and computer skills. And, of course, the infants require less teaching and more individual attention from the child care workers—they ensure that the babies are fed, diapered, and held when awake.

When working with children, child care workers rely on a background in child development to create a flexible schedule allowing time for music, art, play time, academics, rest, and other activities. Depending on the size and structure of the center, workers may be assigned to deal with a particular age group, or they may work with many age groups. Liz Rahl, who holds a bachelor's degree in human development, works as an assistant director for the Discovery Academy, a child care center in Omaha, Nebraska. Her mornings begin with caring for the infants—feeding and diapering them. "My job is to provide comfort," she says. "And hopefully some stimulus." She then works with the preschoolers for most of the morning, returning to the infant room to feed them lunch and put them down for their naps, before returning to the preschoolers to assist them with their lunch. When working with the preschoolers, Rahl helps them to develop skills for kindergarten. "They need to know their numbers, one through 15, and to have alphabet recognition. They need to know how to spell their names and to know their addresses and phone numbers. And their social skills have to be on track for kindergarten. They need to know to share and to take turns and to not talk back." Rahl also works with the children on rhyming and other word skills. "And they need to understand pattern schemes, such as triangle, circle, triangle. Or red, red, blue." To help direct the children, the center organizes a different "theme" every few weeks. The theme may center around a holiday or a season, or a specific letter or number that the children should learn. A nursery rhyme or fairy tale may also be part of the theme.

Workers at a child care center have many responsibilities in addition to giving lessons and instruction. Anyone who has worked with children at all knows they need a lot of assistance in a variety of ways. A major portion of a child care worker's day is spent helping children adjust to being away from home and encouraging them to play together. Children who become frightened or homesick need gentle reassurance. Child care workers often help kids with their coats and boots in the winter and also deal with the sniffles, colds, and generally cranky behavior that can occur in young children. These workers supervise snack time, teaching children how to eat properly and clean up after themselves.

Child care workers also work with the parents of each child. It is not unusual for parents to come to a center and observe a child or go on a field trip with the class, and child care workers often take these opportunities to discuss the progress of each child as well as any specific problems or concerns. Rahl makes sure the parents of the children she cares for are aware of the child's progress. "I send home sheets," she says, "listing any problems along with the good things the kids are doing."

REQUIREMENTS

High School
You should take courses in early childhood development when available. Many home economics courses include units in parenting and child care. English courses will help you to develop communication skills important in dealing with children and their parents. In teaching children, you should be able to draw from a wide base of education and interests, so take courses in art, music, science, and physical education.

Postsecondary Training
A high school diploma and some child care experience is usually all that's required to get a job as a child care worker, but requirements vary among employers. Some employers prefer to hire workers who have taken college courses or hold bachelor's degrees; they may also pay better wages to those with some college education. A college program should include course work in a variety of liberal arts subjects, including English, history, and science, as well as nutrition, child development, psychology of the young child, and sociology. Some employers also offer on-the-job training.

Certification or Licensing
Requirements for child care workers vary from state to state. Each state sets its own licensing requirements for child care workers. Some

states require that you complete a certain number of continuing education hours every year; these hours may include college courses or research into the subject of child care. CPR training is also often required. National certification isn't required of child care workers, but some organizations do offer it. The Council for Professional Recognition offers the Child Development Associate (CDA) National Credentialing Program. To complete the program and receive the CDA credential, you must do a certain amount of field and course work, and pass a final evaluation. According to the council, there are now more than 150,000 CDAs. The National Child Care Association offers the certified childcare professional (CCP) credential. To receive this credential, you must have extensive child care experience, along with special training.

Other Requirements

You should have love and respect for children and a genuine interest in their well-being. You'll also need a great deal of patience and the ability to understand the needs of preschool-aged children in all stages of development. "You need to be able to be on the child's level," Liz Rahl says. "You need to be able to talk directly to them, not down to them." She also emphasizes the importance of a sense of humor. "You need to be laid back, but you can't let them run all over you."

EXPLORING

Talk to neighbors, relatives, and others with small children about baby-sitting some evenings and weekends. Preschools, day care centers, and other child care programs often hire high school students for part-time positions as aides. There are also many volunteer opportunities for working with kids—check with your library or local literacy program about tutoring children and reading to preschoolers. Summer day camps, Bible schools, children's theaters, museums, and other organizations with children's programs also hire high school students as assistants or have need of volunteers.

EMPLOYERS

Both the government and the private sector are working to provide for the enormous need for quality child care. Child care workers should find many job opportunities in private and public preschools, day care centers, government-funded learning programs, religious centers, and Montessori schools. Work is available in small centers or at large centers with many children. Franchisers, like Primrose School Franchising Company and Kids 'R' Kids International, are also providing more employment opportunities. Approximately two out of five child care workers are self-employed.

STARTING OUT

At your first opportunity, you should take part-time work at a child care center to gain firsthand experience. Contact child care centers, nursery schools, Head Start programs, and other preschool facilities to identify job opportunities. The Child Care Bureau estimates that one-third of all child care teachers leave their centers each year. Check the classified section of local newspapers, and you are likely to see many job openings for child care workers. Liz Rahl advises that you get a degree in early child development, so you can advance into a director position if you choose. "And be careful when you choose a child care center," she says. "Make sure you're comfortable with their policies and approaches to child care."

ADVANCEMENT

As child care workers gain experience, they receive salary increases and promotions to such positions as assistant director or preschool teacher. With additional experience and education, they may be able to advance into an administrative position, such as director of a center. Some experienced child care workers with advanced degrees become directors of Head Start programs and other government programs. If a child care worker has a head for business, he or she may choose to open a child care facility. Some child care workers also decide to pursue a degree in education and become certified to teach kindergarten or elementary school.

EARNINGS

Earnings for child care workers depend on their education level, the type of employer, the number of children being cared for, and other such variables. According to the U.S. Department of Labor, the median annual earnings for child care workers in 2002 were $16,950 for full-time work. The department also reports that 10 percent of child care workers earned less than $5.93 per hour (approximately $12,330 annually based on a 40-hour workweek). At the high end of the pay scale, 10 percent of child care workers made more than $12.55 per hour (approximately $26,100 annually based on a 40-

hour workweek). Few child care workers receive full benefits from their employers. Some large day care centers and preschools, however, do offer limited health care coverage and vacation pay.

WORK ENVIRONMENT

Child care workers spend much of their work day on their feet in a classroom or on a playground. Facilities vary from a single room to large buildings. Class sizes also vary; some child care centers serve only a handful of children, while others serve several hundred. Classrooms may be crowded and noisy, but those who love children enjoy all the activity.

Part-time employees generally work between 18 and 30 hours a week, while full-time employees work 35 to 40 hours a week. Part-time work gives the employee flexibility, and for many, this is one of the advantages of the job. "It's a great starter job," Liz Rahl says. The job also allows workers to play with the children and to direct them in games and other activities. "Most adults don't get to have fun at work," she says. She also enjoys watching the children go through all the different stages of development, from infant to preschooler. "It's very rewarding when a preschooler comes in unable to even write a letter," she says, "then soon they're writing their names." Among the children she cares for is her daughter Christa. "The job allows me to be with my child," she says, "so I know what her day's like."

OUTLOOK

Employment is projected to increase about as fast as the average through 2012, according to the U.S. Department of Labor. Job opportunities, however, should be good because there is high turnover in this field, resulting in the need for many replacement workers. One reason for this turnover rate is the low pay; in order to keep quality employees, center owners may have to charge clients more so that they may better compensate staff members. Jobs will also be available as more child care centers, both nonprofit and for-profit, open to meet the increased demand for child care as more mothers take jobs outside the home. There will be more franchises and national chains offering job opportunities to child care workers, as well as centers that cater exclusively to corporate employees. Child care workers may be working with older children, as more day care centers expand to include elementary school services. Bilingual child care workers will find more job opportunities and better salaries.

FOR MORE INFORMATION

For information about certification, contact
Council for Professional Recognition
2460 16th Street, NW
Washington, DC 20009-3575
Tel: 800-424-4310
http://www.cdacouncil.org

Visit the NAEYC website to read relevant articles concerning issues of child care and to learn about membership and accreditation for programs.
National Association for the Education of Young Children (NAEYC)
1509 16th Street, NW
Washington, DC 20036
Tel: 800-424-2460
http://www.naeyc.org

For information about student memberships and training opportunities, contact
National Association of Child Care Professionals
PO Box 90723
Austin, TX 78709-0723
Tel: 800-537-1118
Email: admin@naccp.org
http://www.naccp.org

For information about certification and to learn about the issues affecting child care, visit the NCCA webpage, or contact
National Child Care Association (NCCA)
2025 M Street, NW, Suite 800
Washington, DC 20036-3309
Tel: 202-367-1133
Email: info@nccanet.org
http://www.nccanet.org

Child Life Specialists

QUICK FACTS

School Subjects
Health
Psychology

Personal Skills
Communication/ideas
Helping/teaching

Work Environment
Primarily indoors
Primarily one location

Minimum Education Level
Bachelor's degree

Salary Range
$12,500 to $40,920 to
$70,000

Certification or Licensing
Recommended

Outlook
About as fast as the average

DOT
195

GOE
12.02.02

NOC
N/A

O*NET-SOC
21-1021.00

OVERVIEW

Child life specialists work in health care settings to help infants, children, adolescents, and their families through illness or injury. One of the primary roles of the child life specialist is to ease the anxiety and stress that often accompany hospitalization, injury, or routine medical care. Child life specialists help children, adolescents, and their families maintain living patterns that are as close to normal as possible, and they try to minimize the potential trauma of hospitalization. Child life specialists do this by providing opportunities for play and relaxation, interaction with other children, and personalized attention. They also encourage family involvement, which can play a major role in helping children and adolescents cope with difficult situations. Child life specialists may help children and their families to develop coping skills and educate them about the experience that they are going through.

Some hospitals refer to their child life specialists as *play therapists, patient activity therapists, activity therapists,* or *therapeutic recreation specialists.*

HISTORY

At one time physicians and nurses were the only adults responsible for the care of children in hospitals. Parents left their children in hospitals, frequently for long periods of time, for treatment of their illnesses. But many parents felt that their children's emotional needs were not being met. Children were often not told about what tests, treatments, or procedures they were to undergo, and as a result their hospital experience was frequently traumatic. In addition, social workers who were part of the health care team sometimes were not

22

specially trained to work with children and could not provide them with support.

During the early 20th century attempts were made to improve health care workers' understanding of children's needs and to make hospital stays less emotionally difficult for children. C. S. Mott Hospital in Ann Arbor, Michigan, for example, created the nation's first child life department, focusing on child development, in 1922. Gradually, during the 1940s and 1950s, "play programs" were developed at various care facilities across the country. In these settings children were allowed to relax, play, and feel safe. As professional interest in and understanding of child development grew, the play programs began to be seen not only as a play time but also as a therapeutic part of children's care during hospital stays. During the 1960s and 1970s the field of child life grew dramatically as it gained increasing acceptance.

The profession of child life specialists was formally recognized in 1974, when the Association for the Care of Children's Health formed a committee for child life and activity specialists. The committee, which became the independent organization Child Life Council (CLC) in 1982, had as its goals to promote the profession of child life specialist as well as to strengthen these specialists' professional identity. The committee's members recognized that the interruption of a hospitalization or even an ambulatory procedure can have negative consequences for children's growth and development. Today, child life specialists are recognized as an integral part of a child's health care team.

THE JOB

When children are hospitalized, the experience can be frightening. Child life specialists need to be tuned into the child's or adolescent's concerns. For some children, separation from their families and the familiarity of home can be traumatic. For others, repeated blood tests, needles, or painful procedures can cause fears or nightmares. Emotional damage can be a danger even for adolescents. No matter how short or long the hospital stay and no matter how serious the illness or injury, children can experience anxiety or other emotional effects.

Child life specialists try to ease the possible trauma of being in the hospital. They play an important role in educating and comforting both the patients and their families. They become familiar and trusted adults, and they are usually the only professionals who do not perform tests on the children.

Child life specialists may use dolls and medical instruments to show children what the doctor will be doing. They may help children act out their concerns by having them give a doll a shot if they receive one. The child life specialist may use recreational activities, art projects, cooking, music, and outdoor play in their work. Programs are tailored to meet the needs of individual patients. Some children are unable to express their fears and concerns and may need the child life specialist to draw them out. Some children rely on the child life specialist to help them understand what is happening to them. Still others need the child life specialist to explain children's emotional outbursts or withdrawal to their families.

When children are hospitalized for a long period of time, child life specialists may accompany them to procedures, celebrate successful treatment, or plan a holiday celebration. Child life specialists may also take children on preadmission orientation and hospital tours. They serve as advocates for children's issues by promoting rooming-in or unrestricted parental or sibling visits. Many child life specialists work in conjunction with local school districts to help children keep up with school while they are in the hospital.

Child life administrators supervise the staffs of child life personnel. In larger hospitals, the administrators work with other hospital administrators to run the child life programs smoothly within the hospital setting.

Child life specialists can turn their patients' hospital stays into a time of growth. Children are very resilient, and with proper care by their entire health team, they can emerge from hospital stays with a sense of accomplishment and heightened self-esteem.

REQUIREMENTS

High School

If you are interested in becoming a child life specialist, you will need to plan on going to college after high school. Therefore, you should take a college preparatory curriculum. As a child life specialist you will need to understand family dynamics, child development, educational play, and basic medical terminology. To help you prepare for this specialty, take psychology and sociology courses and, if available, child development classes. In addition, be sure that your class schedule includes science courses, including health and biology. Because communication is such an important aspect of this work, take English, communication, and speech classes. You may also want to take art, physical education, and drama classes to develop skills that you can use in a variety of therapies, such as play, art, and recreation therapy.

Postsecondary Training

Some colleges or universities offer specific programs in child life, and quite a number of schools offer course work in areas related to child life. Those who attend colleges or universities that do not have specific child life programs should major in another appropriate field, such as child development, psychology, and social work. Do some research before you select a school to attend. The CLC advises those considering this career to look for a school program that has sufficient faculty, a variety of field opportunities, and positive student evaluations. The CLC offers information on both undergraduate and graduate programs at its website, http://www.childlife.org/Students_Educators/academic_programs.htm. Typical classes to take include child psychology, child growth and development, family dynamics, and theories of play. Select a program that offers internships. An internship will give you supervised experience in the field as well as prepare you for future employment.

A child life administrator is usually required to have a master's degree in child development, behavioral psychology, education, or a related field. Graduate-level course work typically includes the areas of administration, research, and advanced clinical issues. Those who wish to be considered for positions as child life administrators must also have work experience supervising staff members, managing budgets, and preparing educational materials.

Certification or Licensing

Certification as a certified child life specialist is available through the CLC's Child Life Certifying Committee. Certification criteria include passing an examination and fulfilling education requirements. Although certification is voluntary, it is highly recommended. Some health care centers will not hire a child life specialist who is not certified.

Other Requirements

To be a successful child life specialist you should enjoy working with people, especially children. You will be part of a health care team, so you must be able to communicate effectively with medical professionals as well as able to communicate with children and their families. You must be creative in order to come up with different ways to explain complicated events, such as a surgery, to a child without frightening him or her. You will also need maturity and emotional stability to deal with situations that may otherwise upset you, such as seeing chronically ill or severely injured children. Those who enjoy this work are able to focus on its positive aspects—helping children and their families through difficult times.

EXPLORING

An excellent way to explore your interest in and aptitude for this work is to volunteer. For volunteer opportunities in medical settings, find out what local hospitals, outpatient clinics, or nursing homes have to offer. Opportunities to work with children are also available through organizations such as Easter Seals, Boy Scouts and Girl Scouts, and Big Brothers/Big Sisters of America. In addition, volunteer or paid positions are available at many summer camps. Baby-sitting, of course, is another way to work with children and earn some extra money. And a good baby-sitter is always in demand, no matter where you live.

Once you are in college you can join the CLC as a student member. Membership includes a subscription to the council's newsletter, which can give you a better understanding of the work of a child life specialist.

EMPLOYERS

Child life specialists work as members of the health care team typically in hospitals. Increasingly, though, specialists are finding employment outside of hospitals at such places as rehabilitation centers, hospices, and ambulatory care facilities. Most child life programs in hospitals are autonomous and report to hospital administrations as other departments and programs do.

Child life programs often work with school programs within hospitals. Specialists may work with teachers to coordinate the curriculum with recreational activities. They also may encourage hospital administrations to provide adequate classroom facilities and highly qualified teachers.

STARTING OUT

Your internship may provide you with valuable contacts that can give you information on job leads. In addition, the career center or placement office of your college or university should be able to help you locate your first job. The CLC offers its members use of a job bank that lists openings at hospitals and clinics. You may also contact hospitals' placement offices directly for information on available positions.

ADVANCEMENT

Becoming certified and keeping up with new developments through continuing education workshops and seminars are the first two steps anyone must take in order to advance in this field. The next step is to get a graduate degree. Advancement possibilities include the positions of child life administrator, assistant director, or director of a child life program. Advanced positions involve management responsibilities, including the overseeing of a staff and coordinating a program's activities. Those in advanced positions must also keep their knowledge up-to-date by completing continuing education, attending professional conferences, and reading professional journals.

EARNINGS

Salaries for child life specialists vary greatly depending on such factors as the region of the country a specialist works in, education level, certification, and the size of the employer. For example, salaries tend to be higher in large metropolitan teaching hospitals than in small community hospitals. In 2000, the Department of Human Development and Family Studies of the University of Alabama-Tuscaloosa conducted a salary survey of child life professionals to determine national salary trends for the field. According to this survey, those just starting out in the field had annual salaries ranging from a low of $12,500 to a high of approximately $55,540. The mean income for this group was approximately $28,560. Those with three to five years of work experience had mean annual earnings of $31,585. Child life specialists with more than 10 years of experience reported salaries ranging from $30,000 to $70,000 annually, with a mean income of approximately $40,920. Those with the highest earnings are usually child life administrators or directors. In addition, those with certification tend to earn more than their noncertified counterparts.

Child life specialists' salaries may be compared to those of social workers. According to the Department of Labor, in 2004, such workers made a median of $35,010 per year, with the bottom 10 percent making $23,470 or less and the top 10 percent making $58,410 or more.

Benefits vary by employer, but they usually include such items as paid vacation and sick days, medical insurance, and retirement plans.

WORK ENVIRONMENT

Child life specialists are members of the health care team in a variety of settings, including hospitals, clinics, and hospice facilities. In most hospitals, the child life specialist works in a special playroom. Sometimes the specialist may go to the child's hospital room. In outpatient facilities, the specialist may work in a waiting room or a designated playroom. According to the American Academy of Pediatrics (AAP), the ratio of child life specialists to children that works well is about one to 15. Child life specialists must be comfortable in hospital settings. They need to adjust easily to being around children who are sick. Since the children and their families need so much support, child life specialists need to be emotionally stable. Their own support network of family and friends should be strong, so that the specialist can get through difficult times at work. Child life specialists may have patients who die, and this can be difficult.

Most child life personnel work during regular business hours, although specialists are occasionally needed on evenings, holidays, or weekends to work with the children. It is important for child life personnel to have hobbies or outside interests to avoid becoming too emotionally drained from the work. The rewards of a child life career are great. Many child life specialists see the direct effects of their work on their patients and on their patients' families. They see anxiety and fear being eased, and they see their patients come through treatments and hospitalizations with a renewed pride.

OUTLOOK

The employment outlook for child life specialists is good. The AAP reports that most hospitals specializing in pediatric care have child life programs. In addition, the number of these programs has doubled since 1965. And although managed-care providers encourage short hospital stays that may result in a reduced need for staffing in hospitals, opportunities for child life specialists are increasing outside of the hospital setting. The possible employers of today and tomorrow include outpatient clinics, rehabilitation centers, hospice programs, and other facilities that may treat children, such as sexual assault centers and centers for abused women and children.

FOR MORE INFORMATION

For current news on issues affecting children's health, visit the AAP's website.
American Academy of Pediatrics (AAP)
141 Northwest Point Boulevard
Elk Grove Village, IL 60007-1098
Tel: 847-434-4000

Email: pedscareer@aap.org
http://www.aap.org

For education, career, and certification information as well as professional publications, contact
Child Life Council
11820 Parklawn Drive, Suite 240
Rockville, MD 20852
Tel: 301-881-7090
Email: clcstaff@childlife.org
http://www.childlife.org

For information on children's health issues and pediatric care, contact
National Association of Children's Hospitals and Related Institutions
401 Wythe Street
Alexandria, VA 22314
Tel: 703-684-1355
Email: mbrsvcs@nachri.org
http://www.childrenshospitals.net

Child Psychologists

QUICK FACTS

School Subjects
Biology
Psychology
Sociology

Personal Skills
Helping/teaching
Technical/scientific

Work Environment
Primarily indoors
Primarily one location

Minimum Education Level
Master's degree

Salary Range
$33,380 to $56,360 to
$96,720

Certification or Licensing
Voluntary (certification)
Required for certain
positions (licensing)

Outlook
Faster than the average

DOT
045

GOE
12.02.02

NOC
4151

O*NET-SOC
19-3031.00

OVERVIEW

Psychologists teach, counsel, conduct research, or administer programs to understand people and help people understand themselves. Psychologists who specialize in the study and treatment of children, adolescents, and their families are referred to as *child psychologists.* They examine individual and group behavior through testing, experimenting, and studying personal histories. Unlike psychiatrists, psychologists are not medical doctors and cannot prescribe medication.

The American Psychological Association (APA) is a professional organization serving the interests of psychologists nationwide. Within the umbrella of the APA are several divisions that promote psychologists who work primarily with children and young adults. One such division, School Psychology, promotes the work of psychologists working in a school setting. Currently, there are about 25,000 school psychologists employed in the United States.

HISTORY

The first syllable in psychology derives from *psyche,* a Greek word meaning soul. The second half of psychology contains the root of the word *logic.* Thus, psychology translates as "the science of the soul."

One of the most famous pioneers in child psychology was Jean Piaget, who is best known for reorganizing the stages of cognitive development. He believed children learn in genetically determined stages that always follow the same order: Sensorimotor (birth to two years), Preoperational (two to seven), Concrete Operational (seven to

11), and Formal Operational (11 years and beyond). His work was influential to other psychologists specializing in child development.

Great interest in child and adolescent psychology prompted the APA to form specific divisions to cater to this growing specialization; currently there are eight. In 1968, the Society of Pediatric Psychology was founded as a forum for psychology professionals providing clinical health care for children, adolescents, and their families.

Another organization related to child psychology is the Society of Clinical Child and Adolescent Psychology. This group promotes the development of evaluation of evidence-based treatments for childhood disorders.

THE JOB

Psychology is both a science and a profession. As a science, it is a systematic approach to the understanding of people and their behavior; as a profession, it is the application of that understanding to help solve human problems. Psychology is a rapidly growing field, and psychologists work on a great variety of problems.

The field of psychology is so vast that no one person can become an expert in all phases of it. The psychologist usually concentrates on one specialty. Many of the specialties, such as child psychology, overlap in subject matter and methodology.

Some *clinical psychologists* work exclusively with children's issues. They concern themselves with a child or adolescent's mental and emotional disorders. They assess and treat problems ranging from normal psychological crises, such as trauma from child abuse, to adolescent rebellion, to extreme conditions, such as severe depression and schizophrenia.

They may be staff members at a child guidance clinic or a treatment center for children at a large general hospital. Clinical psychologists also engage in private practice, seeing clients at offices. Clinical psychologists comprise the largest group of specialists.

School psychologists frequently do diagnosis and remediation. They may engage primarily in preventive and developmental psychology. Many school psychologists are assigned the duty of testing pupils surmised to be exceptional. Other school psychologists work almost entirely with children who have proven to be a problem to themselves or to others and who have been referred for help by teachers or other members of the school system. Many school psychologists are concerned with pupils who reveal various kinds of learning disabilities. School psychologists may also be called upon to work with relationship problems between parents and children.

Developmental psychologists study development of people from birth through adulthood. They describe, measure, and explain age-related changes in behavior, stages of emotional development, universal traits and individual differences, and abnormal changes in development. Many developmental psychologists teach and do research in colleges and universities. Some specialize in programs for children in day care centers, preschools, hospitals, or clinics

Social child psychologists study how people interact with each other and how they are affected by their environment. Social psychology has developed from four sources: sociology, cultural anthropology, psychiatry, and psychology. Social psychologists are interested in individual and group behavior. They study the ways groups influence individuals and vice versa. They study different kinds of groups: ethnic, religious, political, educational, family, and many others. The social psychologist has devised ways to research group nature, attitudes, leadership patterns, and structure.

The *educational psychologist* is concerned primarily with how people teach, learn, and evaluate learning. Many educational psychologists are employed on college or university faculties, and they also conduct research into learning theory. Some, however, are interested in evaluating learning.

A child psychologist observes a young girl. *(Jim Whitmer Photography)*

Many psychologists teach some area of basic psychology in colleges and universities. They are also likely to conduct research and supervise graduate student work in an area of special interest.

Many psychologists find that strong writing skills are helpful in their careers. They may write up the results of research efforts for a scholarly journal. Some prepare papers for presentation at professional association meetings or sometimes write books or articles.

Some psychologists become administrators who direct college or university psychology departments or personnel services programs in a school system or industry. Some become agency or department directors of research in scientific laboratories. They may be promoted to department head in a state or federal government agency.

REQUIREMENTS

High School
Since you will need to continue your education beyond high school in order to become a psychologist, you should enroll in college preparatory courses. Your class schedule should concentrate on English courses, computer science, mathematics, and sciences. Algebra, geometry, and calculus are important to take, as are biology, chemistry, and physics. Naturally you should take social science courses, such as psychology and sociology.

If your high school offers childcare or child development classes, take them! One of the most important characteristics of a child psychologist is that they know and enjoy interacting with children.

A foreign language such as Spanish, would also be helpful in preparation for working with bilingual children and their families.

Postsecondary Training
A master's degree is required to work in this profession, but a doctorate in psychology (Ph.D. or Psy.D.) is recommended. While most new doctorates in the psychology field received a Ph.D., the number of Psy.D. recipients is quickly increasing. While some positions are available to people with a master's degree, they are jobs of lesser responsibility and lower salaries than those open to people with a doctorate.

Psychology is an obvious choice of college major if you are interested in this career, but not all graduate programs require entering students to have a psychology bachelor's degree. Nevertheless, your college studies should include a number of psychology courses, such as experimental psychology, developmental psychology, and abnormal psychology.

Master's degree programs typically take two years to complete. Course work at this level usually involves statistics, ethics, and industrial and organizational content. If you want to work as a school psychologist, you will need to complete a supervised, yearlong internship at a school after receiving your degree.

Some doctoral programs accept students with master's degrees; in other cases, students enter a doctoral program with only a bachelor's degree. Because these entrance requirements vary, you will need to research the programs you are interested in to find out their specific requirements. The doctorate degree typically takes between four and seven years to complete for those who begin their studies with only the bachelor's degree. Coursework will include studies in various areas of psychology and research (including work in quantitative research methods). Those who focus on research often complete a yearlong postdoctoral fellowship. Those who want to work as clinical, counseling, or school psychologists must complete a one-year supervised internship. Frequently those who are interested in clinical, counseling, or school psychology will get the Psy.D. because this degree emphasizes clinical rather than research work. In addition, those interested in these three areas should attend a program accredited by the APA.

Certification or Licensing

The National Association of School Psychologists (NASP) awards the nationally certified school psychologist designation to applicants who complete educational requirements, an internship, and successfully pass an examination.

The American Board of Professional Psychology offers voluntary specialty certification in clinical child and adolescent psychology and school psychology. Requirements for certification include having an APA accredited doctoral education and training, appropriate postdoctoral training, approved internship, and successful examination. Those who fulfill these requirements receive the designation diplomate.

Psychologists in independent practice or those providing any type of patient care, such as clinical, counseling, and school psychologists, must be licensed or certified by the state in which they practice. Some states require the licensing of industrial/organizational psychologists. Because requirements vary, you will need to check with your state's licensing board for specific information.

Other Requirements

Because child psychology can be practiced with many specializations and settings, various personal attributes apply to different positions. Those involved in research, for example, should be analytical, detail oriented, and have strong math and writing skills. Those working with patients should be "people persons," able to relate to others, and have excellent listening skills. No matter what their area of focus, however, all child psychologists should have a desire to help others; especially children who may not be always able to speak out for themselves. They should also be committed to lifelong learning since our understanding of humans is constantly evolving.

EXPLORING

There are plenty of opportunities to explore this exciting field, even while you are in high school. Fill your class schedule with all levels of psychology classes your school has to offer. Enroll in child development classes as well, since knowledge of this topic will surely help in your further studies.

Read, read, and read! Check your school or neighborhood library for books on the subject of psychology, including biographies of noted psychologists and their theories. You can also research on the Web to learn more about mental health issues. Get started with the National Mental Health Association at http://www.nmha.org or the APA at http://www.apa.org.

Volunteering for various organizations and charity events will not only give you valuable career experience, but it also serves as a way to network with important industry contacts. If being involved with patient care interests you, gain experience in the health care field by volunteering at a local hospital, clinic, or shelter. In addition, volunteer or part-time work opportunities may exist at area childcare centers, sports facilities, or community centers. If doing research work sounds appealing to you, consider joining your school's science club, which may offer the opportunity to work on projects, documenting the process, and working as part of a team.

Some experienced child psychologists insist that before you can access what is "abnormal," you must first know normalcy. Gain this knowledge, and practical experience by spending time with children of all ages. You can baby-sit neighborhood children, work part time at a children's library, or volunteer to assist in leading a scout troop. You may even want to consider joining a big brother/big sister organization, which provides children with mentoring and friendship relationships. Call your local YMCA or town hall to see if there are any such organizations nearby.

EMPLOYERS

Child clinical psychologists may work with patients in a private practice, hospital, or community center where they provide therapy after evaluation through special tests.

Many psychologists specialize in developmental psychology and teach or perform research in colleges and universities. Some specialize in programs for children in day care centers, preschools, hospitals, or clinics. Others specialize in the social psychology of children and teach or conduct research in colleges or universities. They also work for agencies of the federal or state government or in private research firms. Some work as consultants.

School psychologists practice in public and private school settings, as well as hospitals, clinics, and in private practice.

Educational psychologists may work for test publishing firms devising and standardizing tests of ability, aptitude, personal preferences, attitudes, or characteristics.

The APA website offers links to potential employers as well as a job section listing employment opportunities nationwide. The NASP website also has a career center which offers opportunities to post your resume, and a list of available school psychology positions.

STARTING OUT

University placement offices or a psychology professor may be able to help students find positions after graduation. In addition, contacts made during an internship may offer job leads. Joining professional organizations and networking with members is also a way to find out about job openings. In addition, these organizations, such as the APA, often offer student memberships and list job vacancies at their website, as well as many publications for members.

ADVANCEMENT

For those who have master's degrees, the first step to professional advancement is to complete a doctorate degree. After that, advancement will depend on the area of child psychology in which the person is working. For example, school psychologists might transfer to larger school districts or become directors of pupil personnel services.

A psychologist teaching at a college or university may advance through the academic ranks from instructor to professor. It is also considered a career advancement to be published in industry journals or other scholarly work. Some college teachers who enjoy administrative work become department heads.

Psychologists who work for state or federal government agencies may, after considerable experience, be promoted to head a section or department. After several years of experience, many psychologists enter private practice or set up their own research or consulting firms.

EARNINGS

Because the psychology field offers so many different types of employment possibilities, salaries for child psychologists vary greatly. In addition, the typical conditions affecting salaries, such as the person's level of education, professional experience, and location, also apply. The U.S. Department of Labor reports that clinical, counseling, and school psychologists earned median salaries of $56,360 in 2004. Salaries ranged from less than $33,380 to $96,720 or more. The department also reports the following mean annual earnings for clinical, counseling, and school psychologists by employer: elementary/secondary schools, $61,930; offices of other health practitioners, $78,400; individual and family services, $52,480; offices of physicians, $91,900; and outpatient care centers, $52,900.

WORK ENVIRONMENT

Child psychologists work under many different conditions. Offices of school psychologists may be located in the school system headquarters. They may see students and their parents at those offices, or they might work in space set aside for them in several schools within the school district that they may visit regularly.

Some child psychologists are self-employed. Most work as clinical psychologists and have offices where they see clients. Others work as consultants to business firms. Those who are self-employed rent or own their office spaces and arrange their own work schedules.

Child psychologists employed in government work in such diverse places as public health facilities or state departments of education. Their working conditions depend largely on the kind of jobs they have. They may work mainly with children and their families or be assigned entirely to research.

Those who work as college or university teachers usually have offices in a building on campus and access to a "laboratory" in which they carry out experiments.

OUTLOOK

The U.S. Department of Labor projects that employment for child psychologists will grow faster than the average through 2012, with the largest increase in schools, hospitals, social service agencies, mental health centers, consulting firms, and private companies. Increased emphasis on health maintenance and illness prevention as well as growing interest in psychological services and early intervention for children will create demand for child psychologists. Many of these areas depend on government funding, however, and could be adversely affected in an economic downswing when spending is likely to be curtailed. Prospects look best for doctorate holders in applied areas, such as clinical, counseling, and school psychology.

FOR MORE INFORMATION

For information on specialty certification, contact
American Board of Professional Psychology
300 Drayton Street, 3rd Floor
Savannah, GA 31401
Tel: 800-255-7792
Email: office@abpp.org
http://www.abpp.org

For more on careers in child psychology, related specialty divisions, and voluntary certification, contact
American Psychological Association
750 First Street, NE
Washington, DC 20002-4242
Tel: 800-374-2721
http://www.apa.org

For licensing information, contact
Association of State and Provincial Psychology Boards
PO Box 241245
Montgomery, AL 36124-1245
Tel: 334-832-4580
Email: asppb@asppb.org
http://www.asppb.org

For more information on certification and becoming a school psychologist, including graduate school information, contact
National Association of School Psychologists
4340 East-West Highway, Suite 402
Bethesda, MD 20814

Tel: 301-657-0270
Email: center@nasweb.org
http://www.nasponline.org

*For a list of Canadian psychology departments providing graduate
programs, contact*
Canadian Psychological Association
141 Laurier Avenue West, Suite 702
Ottawa, ON K1P 5J3
Tel: 613-237-2144
Email: cpa@cpa.ca
http://www.cpa.ca

For a whimsical introduction to psychology, visit
ePsych
http://epsych.msstate.edu

*For career information and a list of graduate programs in child
psychology, visit the following website:*
Society of Clinical Child and Adolescent Psychology
http://www.wjh.harvard.edu/~nock/Div53

*For information on financial aid and a list of graduate programs in
child psychology, visit the following website:*
Society of Pediatric Psychology
http://www.apa.org/divisions/div54

INTERVIEW

*Tammy Taylor is a certified school psychologist in the Plainfield Com-
munity Consolidated School District 202 in Plainfield, Illinois. She
has been a child psychologist since 2004. Tammy was kind enough to
discuss her career with the editors of* Careers in Focus: Child Care.

Q. What are your main duties as a child psychologist?

A. I serve as the building psychologist for an early childhood learning center and a middle school, with 850 and 1,300 students
enrolled, respectively. At the early childhood learning center, I
have the added responsibility of working for the district's Child
Find team. This team is charged with screening and identifying
children ages three to six in the school district who may need
special education services. I am not involved in the screen-
ings, and I am only needed for assessments when the child is
suspected of being on the Autism Spectrum or if they are five

years old. The assessments may be either play-based (for the three- and four-year-olds) or formal, standardized testing for the older children. I participate in approximately five to 10 of these per month.

At the early childhood learning center, I also complete any necessary standardized assessments of children who are in need of reevaluations to determine continued eligibility for special education. The formalized evaluations typically consist of a standardized measure of cognitive ability, such as the Wechsler Preschool and Primary Scale of Intelligence-Third Edition and an achievement measure (e.g., the Young Children's Achievement Test). These results are then used to determine special education eligibility based upon federal and state regulations. The meetings to determine eligibility are called Multi-Disciplinary Conferences (MDCs) and involve the child's parents, educational team, any necessary support personnel (e.g., school psychologist, social worker, speech pathologist, occupational therapist, physical therapist, etc.), and an administrator. The administrator is responsible for facilitating the meeting at the early learning center.

My job duties are essentially the same at the middle school I serve, but students who are in need of special education services are identified through a referral process (either the parent or educational team can make the referral) rather than a Child Find team. A major difference between my job duties at both schools is that, at the middle school, I typically run all of the initial case study MDC meetings and reevaluation meetings. I also schedule all of these meetings and complete much of the paperwork necessary to the process. These tasks are done by the administrators, secretary, and/or teachers at the early childhood center.

Q. What are the most important personal and professional qualities for child psychologists?

A. The single most important quality, both personally and professionally, is that a child/school psychologist must like children. Personal qualities that are important:
- compassion
- integrity
- good interpersonal skills
- multitasking skills

Professional qualities that are important:
- organizational skills

- good time-management skills
- an ability to consult with others and facilitate discussions
- problem-solving abilities/creative thinking skills
- writing skills (we write MANY reports)
- communication skills
- a desire to continue learning more as the field changes in scope

Q. What are some of the pros and cons of your job?
A. Pros
  - I am able to work with children in an educational setting.
  - Autonomy (I set my own schedule within the time frame of school hours).
  - I can help students, parents, and teachers.
  - Summers off.
  - Salary.

Cons
  - Paperwork.
  - Not enough time in the day to do everything (even working after school hours).
  - Too many kids to help and not enough resources (often) to do that as effectively as I would like.
  - Our district is large, and there is not enough consistency between the schools, which would help in delivering services more effectively.
  - As a psychologist, people (teachers) naturally vent and complain to me about things, which can become a bit frustrating after awhile.

Q. What is the future employment outlook for child psychologists?
A. Three or four years ago, *U.S. News & World Report* listed school psychology as one of the top 10 fields with the best job prospects. At this time, the field is experiencing a shortage of qualified school psychologists. Currently, our role is being redefined within the schools, and psychologists will soon be less involved with formal evaluations and more occupied with more flexible ways to deliver services to all students who struggle academically and behaviorally in school. There has been talk that this may result in less need for school psychologists, but, currently, this does not seem to be the case.

Children's Librarians

QUICK FACTS

School Subjects
Computer science
English

Personal Skills
Helping/teaching
Leadership/management

Work Environment
Primarily indoors
Primarily one location

Minimum Education Level
Master's degree

Salary Range
$29,890 to $46,940 to
$71,270

Certification or Licensing
Required by certain states

Outlook
About as fast as the average

DOT
100

GOE
12.03.04

NOC
5111

O*NET-SOC
25-4021.00

OVERVIEW

Children's librarians oversee the daily operations of the children's department of public and private libraries and school libraries. They purchase books, periodicals, music and films, and other informational material, and prepare them for circulation. Children's librarians also serve as instructors and mentors to students. In addition, they conduct activities to introduce children to different types of literature. These activities include story time, reading challenges, book discussions, and outreach projects. Approximately 167,000 librarians (including children's librarians) are employed in the United States.

HISTORY

Since ancient times, libraries have been centers where adults could learn, read, and access information. But until the 19th century, no libraries devoted sections to the specific needs and interests of children.

Library historians disagree on when the first public library in the United States that featured resources for children was founded. In 1837, the Arlington (Massachusetts) Public Library became one of the first libraries to offer access to children, according to *The World Wide School,* by Alice Hazeltine. Families could check out as many as three books and keep them for 30 days. They were even allowed to pull books from the shelves until a change in the library's charter stated that "no person except the librarian shall remove a book from the shelves."

During the 1830s, school district libraries also began to appear in New York and New England and eventually spread throughout the country. Materials in these libraries were typically geared toward assisting students to write papers and study for tests.

By the late 1890s and early 1900s, public libraries with children's sections were founded in several major U.S. cities. The Children's Librarian Section of the American Library Association was founded in 1901 to support this new library specialty. During these years, school districts and individual schools also continued to improve their library services. The American Association of School Librarians was founded in 1951, but it traces its origins to the early 1910s via various children-oriented discussion groups and roundtables facilitated by its parent organization, the American Library Association.

Today, children's libraries feature not only books, but periodicals, videotapes, DVDs, films, maps, photographs, music, toys, games, puzzles, and a variety of other useful resources for children.

THE JOB

Many libraries have special departments that cater to children. This library within a library, often called a children's library, houses collections of age-appropriate fiction and nonfiction, as well as research tools such as encyclopedias and atlases. They may also have computers that feature programs and games that appeal to the young and more traditional toys and puzzles. Oftentimes, librarians choose to work with a particular age group. Those who work specifically with children and young adults are referred to as *children's librarians* or *youth services librarians*. If employed in a school setting, such librarians are called *library media specialists*. Regardless of title, children's librarians help young library patrons find and select information best suited to their needs, whether for school research, personal knowledge, or simply the enjoyment of reading a book or finding a useful or entertaining resource.

Maintaining and organizing library facilities are the primary responsibilities of children's librarians. One major task is selecting and ordering books and other media, including fiction and nonfiction, reference books such as encyclopedias and dictionaries, study guides, maps, periodicals, videos, DVDs, and music. These materials must be organized so library patrons can access them easily. New acquisitions are cataloged in card files by title, author, and subject matter. More often, cataloging is computerized. Each book is given a label and card pocket, and stamped with the library's name and address. A bar code is attached to help keep track of its location. Children's librarians must regularly inventory their collection to locate lost or overdue books, identify books that need repairs, or to dispose of outdated or worn materials.

Libraries are given an annual budget by either the school board or library board. Children's librarians must consider this budget when making new purchases or additions to the collection. When the budget allows, they fulfill special book requests from children, teachers, or parents.

Children's librarians are teachers as well. They have a thorough knowledge of their library's collection so they can effectively help students with any research questions, or guide them towards a reading selection suited for their grade or reading level. They are familiar with the works of established authors, as well as newly published books and series. Children's librarians also teach effective ways to navigate library resources using the Dewey Decimal System, online catalog systems, or research on the Internet. They work with area schools and teachers to help plan and organize upcoming class projects and tests. Many times, they provide instruction to patrons and students on the use of library equipment—computers, audiovisual equipment, copy machines, or computer programs.

The implementation of special projects is also a major responsibility of children's librarians. They host story time for toddlers and preschool-aged children, often planning a special craft project related to the day's story. Children's librarians often schedule holiday parties and puppet shows. They may offer school-age children summer reading programs and challenges, author visits, or book clubs.

Children's librarians also organize displays of books, artwork, collections, or memorabilia that may be of interest to children. They are responsible for soliciting the display of private collections and setting up and dismantling the displays. They create a comfortable and inviting space that is appealing to children of all ages using colorful furniture and cozy reading areas. They also decorate the library with book displays, posters, toys, and seasonal items.

Children's librarians are also responsible for outreach services such as the book mobile. These mini-libraries house a collection of books and periodicals that travel to different locations in the community. Library employees staff the book mobile and often conduct a story and craft time for the children. Children's librarians may also promote library services at area preschools via story telling, book totes, and bookmarks.

Children's librarians also have management duties. They supervise library technicians and nonprofessional staff such as clerks, student workers, or volunteers. They often train staff regarding the layout of the library, use of special equipment, or new computer programs.

REQUIREMENTS

High School

A full academic course load—including history, math, English, speech, and computer science—is your best preparation for a career as a children's librarian. Familiarity with the Dewey Decimal System is important—it is important to be able to navigate your way around a library. Also, join clubs or find activities that will give you plenty of experience playing and working with children. Examples of this include taking high school child development courses, baby-sitting neighborhood children, or volunteering at a summer camp or after school program for kids. Don't forget to nurture your love of books, so read, read, read!

Postsecondary Training

A master's degree in library science from an accredited school is required for most children's librarian positions in public libraries. Library Management, Youth Services Librarianship, Literature and Resources Children, and History of Children's Literature are just some of the typical courses that students take for this degree. Workshops covering topics such as electronic publishing and library materials and services for very young children are offered to complement more traditional educational programs.

Those employed in a school setting can take a different route to this career. Some schools require their librarians to be licensed teachers before receiving training or certification in library science. Requirements differ by state. You can check your state's requirements at websites such as the University of Kentucky College of Education's Website, http://www.uky.edu/Education/TEP/usacert.html. The site lists education and training requirements for each state, which is especially helpful if you plan on working as a children's librarian in another state during your career.

Certification or Licensing

Children's librarians in some states may be required to earn teacher's certification and/or a master's degree in addition to preparation as a librarian. Education and certification requirements vary by state, county, and local governments. Contact the school board or public library system in your area to learn about specific requirements.

Other Requirements

Children's librarians should enjoy working with children. They must be good teachers and have the patience to explain library services and technology to children of varying ages and levels of understanding.

Children's librarians should also have strong interpersonal skills, the ability to solve problems, and be detail-oriented. They must also love information and be committed to pursuing continuing education throughout their careers.

EXPLORING

Volunteering to work in your school library is an excellent way to learn more about this career. Many schools rely on students to assist school librarians. As a media center aide, you may be asked to staff the library checkout desk, shelve returned books and periodicals, or maintain audiovisual equipment. Volunteering or working part time at your local library is the ideal way to explore this career. You can get hands-on experience with the working routine of a real library and network for future job opportunities.

Don't forget to visit websites of library associations such as the American Library Association, the Association for Library Services for Children, and the American Association of School Librarians. These organization's sites can provide a wealth of information about education programs, scholarships, financial aid, certification, and student membership.

EMPLOYERS

Approximately 167,000 librarians are employed in the United States. Children's librarians are employed by public and private libraries and elementary and secondary schools.

ADVANCEMENT

Experienced children's librarians may advance by taking a position in a larger school district or in a larger library system. Others, with additional education, may become library directors or library educators.

Some children's librarians pursue careers in other fields. Children's author Beverly Cleary and first lady Laura Bush are two examples of famous former children's librarians. Others may use their experience in the field to work as consultants to publishing companies.

EARNINGS

Salaries for children's librarians depend on such factors as the size, location, and type of library; the responsibilities of the position; and the amount of experience the librarian has. According to the

U.S. Department of Labor, median annual earnings of librarians were $46,940 in 2004. Ten percent of all librarians earned less than $29,890, and 10 percent earned $71,270 or more annually. Librarians working in elementary and secondary schools earned mean annual salaries of $49,670 in 2004. Librarians employed by local government earned mean annual salaries of $45,220 in 2004.

Most librarians receive compensated sick leave, paid vacation time, and holiday pay, are covered by various insurance plans, and take part in retirement savings programs.

WORK ENVIRONMENT

Most children's librarians work a 40-hour week, with hours scheduled depending on the operational time of the main library or school. Some librarians prefer to work part time. The work environment, whether at a library or school, is comfortable and pleasant. Libraries, especially those designated for children, are usually colorfully decorated with many workspaces and cozy reading nooks. Most libraries are open from early in the morning until evening and keep weekend hours as well. Librarians employed in a school setting usually have the same work hours as teachers and receive time off during summer and spring breaks and teacher institute days. Library media specialists report directly to the principal of their school; those employed at a public library report to the library director.

OUTLOOK

The U.S. Department of Labor predicts that employment for librarians, including children's librarians, will grow about as fast as the average over the next decade. This specialty is a popular choice for many aspiring librarians, which means that competition for the best jobs will remain strong over the next decade. Children's librarians who are willing to relocate or take lesser-paying positions in rural areas will have the best employment prospects.

FOR MORE INFORMATION

For career information and a list of accredited educational programs, contact
American Association of School Librarians
c/o American Library Association
50 East Huron Street
Chicago, IL 60611

Tel: 800-545-2433, ext. 4382
Email: AASL@ala.org
http://www.ala.org/aasl

For information on careers, accredited schools, and college student membership, contact
American Library Association
50 East Huron Street
Chicago, IL 60611
Tel: 800-545-2433
Email: library@ala.org
http://www.ala.org

For information on a career as a children's librarian, contact
Association for Library Service to Children
50 East Huron Street
Chicago, IL 60611
Tel: 800-545-2433, ext. 2163
Email: alsc@ala.org
http://www.ala.org/ala/alsc/alsc.htm

━━━━━━━━ INTERVIEW ━━━━━━━━

Jackie Carone is the head of children's services at the Elwood Public Library in East Northport, New York. She has been a children's librarian since September 2002. Jackie was kind enough to discuss her career with the editors of Careers in Focus: Child Care.

Q. **Why did you decide to become a children's librarian?**
A. I absolutely adore working with children, teaching, doing research, reading, and learning new things. Being a children's librarian allows me to do all of these things.

Q. **What are your typical tasks/responsibilities as a children's librarian?**
A. I am the head of children's services, so my responsibilities might be a little different than a regular children's librarian. I decide what items we will purchase for the collection, weed the collection to make room for more items, answer patrons' questions, find information, schedule part-time librarians, supervise pages, plan programs, perform storytimes, do outreach services at local hospitals and medical centers, and attend appropriate workshops and educational courses to improve my skills.

Q. What are the three most important professional qualities for children's librarians?

A. I feel that the three most important professional qualities for children's librarians are enjoying working with children, having excellent people skills, and having knowledge of children's learning and development.

Q. What advice would you give to high school students who are interested in this career?

A. Volunteer or become a page at your local library so you can see what really happens during a typical day. Read, read, read!

Coaches

QUICK FACTS

School Subjects
English
Physical education

Personal Skills
Communication/ideas
Helping/teaching

Work Environment
Indoors and outdoors
Primarily multiple locations

Minimum Education Level
Some postsecondary training

Salary Range
$13,270 to $25,930 to
$56,740

Certification or Licensing
Required in certain positions

Outlook
About as fast as the average

DOT
153

GOE
01.10.01

NOC
5252

O*NET-SOC
27-2022.00

OVERVIEW

Coaches work with a single, organized team or individual, teaching the skills associated with that sport. A coach prepares her or his team for competition and, during the competition, continues to give instruction from a vantage point near the court or playing field.

HISTORY

For as long as there have been individual and team sports, there have been coaches—both informal and those hired by a school or community organization—to teach young people the often intricate skills associated with athletics. As school athletics become more organized, and become available to children of younger ages, coaches will continue to be needed to teach sports-related skills and serve as role models.

THE JOB

The specific job requirements of coaches vary according to the type of sport and the types of people they teach. For example, a coach teaching flag football to a team of 14-year-olds will have different duties and responsibilities than a coach teaching tee-ball to a group of five-year-olds. Nevertheless, all coaches are teachers. They must be very knowledgeable about rules and strategies for their respective sports, but without an effective teaching method that reinforces correct techniques and procedures, their players won't be able to share that valuable knowledge. Also, coaches need to be aware of and open to new procedures and techniques. Many attend clinics or seminars to learn more about their sport or even how to teach more effectively. Many are members of professional organizations that deal exclusively with their sport.

Safety is a primary concern for all coaches. Coaches make sure their students have the right equipment and know its correct use. A major component of safety is helping students feel comfortable and confident with their abilities. This entails teaching the proper stances, techniques, and movements of a game, instructing students on basic rules, and answering any questions.

Coaches use lectures and demonstrations to show young people the proper skills, and both point out the mistakes or deficiencies of individuals.

Motivation is another key element in sports coaching. Almost all sports require stamina, and most coaches will tell you that psychological preparation is every bit as important as physical training. The level of motivation used may differ greatly by the age group the coach is instructing. For example, motivation and psychological preparation may be incorporated into an instructional session with a freshman basketball team, whose members have the intellectual maturity to grasp these concepts. Coaches of younger children might skip these concepts and focus on stressing the importance of teamwork, good sportsmanship, and simply the fun and excitement of playing a sport regardless of the individual's talent level.

REQUIREMENTS

Training and educational requirements vary, depending on the specific sport and the ability level of students being instructed. Most coaches who are associated with schools have bachelor's degrees. Many middle and high school coaches are also teachers within the school.

High School

To prepare for college courses, high school students should take courses that teach human physiology. Biology, health, and exercise classes would all be helpful. Courses in English and speech are also important to improve or develop communication skills.

There is no substitute for developing expertise in a sport. If you can play the sport well and effectively explain to other people how they might play as well as you, you will most likely be able to get a job as a sports coach. The most significant source of training for this occupation is gained while on the job.

A volleyball coach discusses strategy with two of her players. *(Jim Whitmer Photography)*

Postsecondary Training

Postsecondary training in this field varies greatly. College and professional coaches often attended college as athletes, while others attended college and received their degrees without playing a sport. If you are interested in becoming a middle school or high school coach, you will need a college degree because you will most likely be teaching as well as coaching. At the middle school or high school level, coaches spend their days teaching everything from physical education to English to mathematics, so the college courses these coaches take vary greatly. Coaches of some youth league sports may not need a postsecondary degree, but they must have a solid understanding of their sport and of injury prevention.

Certification or Licensing

Since most middle school and high school coaches also work as teachers, people interested in this job should plan to obtain teacher certification in their state.

Other Requirements

Coaches have to be experts in their sport. They must have complete knowledge of the rules and strategies of the game, so that they can creatively design effective plays and techniques for their athletes. But the requirements for this job do not end here. Sports coaches should enjoy working with a wide variety of people. They should be able to communicate clearly and possess good leadership skills to effectively teach complex skills. They can take pride in the knowledge that they have helped their students or their players reach new heights of achievement and training.

Coaches must also be able to work under pressure, guiding teams through games and tournaments that carry great personal stakes for everyone involved.

EXPLORING

Try to gain as much experience as possible in all sports and a specific sport in particular. It is never too early to start. High school and college offer great opportunities to participate in sporting events either as a player, manager, trainer, or in intramural leagues.

Most communities have sports programs such as Little League baseball or track and field meets sponsored by the recreation commission. Get involved by volunteering as a coach, umpire, or starter.

Talking with sports coaches already working in the field is also a good way to discover specific job information and find out about career opportunities.

EMPLOYERS

Besides working in middle schools and high schools, coaches are hired by colleges and universities, professional sports teams, individual athletes such as tennis players, and by youth leagues, summer camps, and recreation centers.

STARTING OUT

People with expertise in a particular sport who are interested in becoming a coach or instructor, should apply directly to the appropriate facility. Sometimes a facility will provide training.

Many colleges also offer positions to *graduate assistant coaches.* Graduate assistant coaches are recently graduated players who are interested in becoming coaches. They receive a stipend and gain valuable coaching experience.

ADVANCEMENT

Advancement opportunities for coaches depend on the individual's skills, willingness to learn, and work ethic. Some would argue that, for professional coaches, a high percentage of wins is the only criterion for success. However coaches in the scholastic ranks have other responsibilities and other factors that measure success. High school and college coaches must make sure their players are getting good grades, and middle school coaches can be successful if they produce a team that competes in a sportsmanlike fashion regardless of whether they win or lose.

Successful coaches are often hired by larger schools. High school coaches may advance to become college coaches, and the most successful college coaches often are given the opportunity to coach professional teams. Former players sometimes land assistant or head coaching positions.

EARNINGS

The U.S. Department of Labor reports that the median earnings for sports coaches and scouts were $25,930 in 2004. The lowest 10 percent earned less than $13,270, while the highest 10 percent earned more than $56,740. Sports coaches who worked at colleges and universities earned a mean annual salary of $42,420 in 2004, while those employed by elementary and secondary schools earned $27,000.

Most coaches who work at the high school level or below also teach within the school district. Besides their teaching salary and coaching fee—either a flat rate or a percentage of their annual salary—school coaches receive a benefits package that includes paid vacations and health insurance.

WORK ENVIRONMENT

Coaches work in a variety of settings—from snow-covered football fields to climate-controlled gyms. Coaches who work as middle school or high school teachers work regular school hours, but may occasionally work a total of 12 to 16 hours a day, five or six days each week as a result of practices, tournaments, and other events. Coaches who are employed by community organizations typically work part time.

OUTLOOK

According to the U.S. Department of Labor, this occupation will grow about as fast as the average through 2012. Coaching jobs at the middle school, high school, and amateur level will be plentiful as long as the public continues its fascination with sports and focus on fitness. The creation of new professional leagues, as well as the expansion of current leagues will open some new employment opportunities for professional coaches, but competition for these jobs will be very intense. There will also be openings as other coaches retire, or are terminated. However, there is very little job security in professional coaching, unless a coach can consistently produce a winning team.

FOR MORE INFORMATION

For trade journals, job listings, and a list of graduate schools, visit the AAHPERD website.
    American Alliance for Health, Physical Education, Recreation and Dance (AAHPERD)
    1900 Association Drive
    Reston, VA 20191-1598
    Tel: 800-213-7193
    http://www.aahperd.org

For information on membership and baseball coaching education, coaching Web links, and job listings, visit the ABCA website.
    American Baseball Coaches Association (ABCA)
    108 South University Avenue, Suite 3
    Mount Pleasant, MI 48858-2327
    Tel: 989-775-3300
    Email: abca@abca.org
    http://www.abca.org

For information on careers in sports and physical education, contact
    National Association for Sport and Physical Education
    1900 Association Drive
    Reston, VA 20191-1598
    Tel: 800-213-7193
    Email: naspe@aahperd.org
    http://www.aahperd.org/naspe

For information on high school coaching opportunities, contact
    National High School Athletic Coaches Association
    Norwich Free Academy
    305 Broadway
    Norwich, CT 06360
    Tel: 860-425-5512
    Email: office@hscoaches.org
    http://www.hscoaches.org

Creative Arts Therapists

QUICK FACTS

School Subjects
Art
Music
Theater/dance

Personal Skills
Artistic
Helping/teaching

Work Environment
Primarily indoors
Primarily one location

Minimum Education Level
Master's degree

Salary Range
$15,000 to $42,000 to
$100,000

Certification or Licensing
Required by all states

Outlook
About as fast as the average

DOT
076

GOE
14.06.01

NOC
3144

O*NET-SOC
N/A

OVERVIEW

Creative arts therapists treat and rehabilitate people with mental, physical, and emotional disabilities. They use the creative processes of music, art, dance/movement, drama, psychodrama, and poetry in their therapy sessions to determine the underlying causes of problems and to help patients achieve therapeutic goals. Creative arts therapists usually specialize in one particular type of therapeutic activity. The specific objectives of the therapeutic activities vary according to the needs of the patient and the setting of the therapy program.

HISTORY

Creative arts therapy programs are fairly recent additions to the health care field. Although many theories of mental and physical therapy have existed for centuries, health care professionals have realized the healing powers of music, art, dance, and other forms of artistic self-expression only in the last 70 years or so.

Art therapy is based on the idea that people who can't discuss their problems with words must have another outlet for self-expression. In the early 1900s, psychiatrists began to look more closely at their patients' artwork, realizing that there could be links between the emotional or psychological illness and the art. Sigmund Freud even did some preliminary research into the artistic expression of his patients.

In the 1930s, art educators discovered that children often expressed their thoughts better with pictures and role-playing than they did through verbalization. Children often don't know the words they need to explain how they feel or how to make their needs known to adults. Researchers began to look into art as a way to treat children who were traumatized by abuse, neglect, illness, or other physical or emotional disabilities.

During and after World War II, the Department of Veterans Affairs (VA) developed and organized various art, music, and dance activities for patients in VA hospitals. These activities had a dramatic effect on the physical and mental well-being of World War II veterans. Based on the success of these programs, creative arts therapists began to help treat and rehabilitate patients in other health care settings.

Because of early breakthroughs with children and veterans, the number of arts therapists has increased greatly over the past few decades, and the field has expanded to include drama, psycho-drama, and poetry, in addition to the original areas of music, art, and dance. Today, creative arts therapists work with diverse populations of patients in a wide range of facilities, and they focus on the specific needs of a vast spectrum of disorders and disabilities. Colleges and universities offer degree programs in many types of therapies, and national associations for registering and certifying creative arts therapists work to monitor training programs and to ensure the professional integrity of the therapists working in the various fields.

THE JOB

Creative arts therapy taps into the subconscious and gives people a mode of expression in an uncensored environment. This is important because before patients can begin to heal, they must first identify their feelings. Once they recognize their feelings, they can begin to develop an understanding of the relationship between their feelings and their behavior.

The main goal of a creative arts therapist is to improve the client's physical, mental, and emotional health. Before therapists begin any treatment, they meet with a team of other health care professionals. After determining the strength, limitations, and interests of their client, they create a program to promote positive change and growth. The creative arts therapist continues to confer with the other health care workers as the program progresses, and alters the program according to the client's progress. How these goals are reached depends on the unique specialty of the therapist in question.

"It's like sitting in the woods waiting for a fawn to come out." That is how Barbara Fish, former Director of Activity Therapy for the Illinois Department of Mental Health and Developmental Disabilities, Chicago Metropolitan and Adolescent Services, describes her experience as she waits patiently for a sexually abused patient to begin to trust her. The patient is extraordinarily frightened because of the traumatic abuse she has suffered. This may be the first time in the patient's life that she is in an environment of acceptance and support. It may take months or even years before the patient begins to trust the therapist, "come out of the woods," and begin to heal.

In some cases, especially when the clients are adolescents, they may have become so detached from their feelings that they can physically act out without consciously knowing the reasons for their behavior. This detachment from their emotions creates a great deal of psychological pain. With the help of a creative arts therapist, clients can begin to communicate their subconscious feelings both verbally and nonverbally. They can express their emotions in a variety of ways without having to name them.

Creative arts therapists work with all age groups: young children, adolescents, adults, and senior citizens. They can work in individual, group, or family sessions. The approach of the therapist, however, depends on the specific needs of the client or group. For example, if an individual is feeling overwhelmed by too many options or stimuli, the therapist may give him or her only a plain piece of paper and a pencil to work with that day.

Fish has three ground rules for her art therapy sessions with disturbed adolescents: respect yourself, respect other people, and respect property. The therapy groups are limited to five patients per group. She begins the session by asking each person in the group how he or she is feeling that day. By carefully listening to their responses, a theme may emerge that will determine the direction of the therapy. For example, if anger is reoccurring in their statements, Fish may ask them to draw a line down the center of a piece of paper. On one side, she will ask them to draw how anger looks and on the other side how feeling sad looks. Then, once the drawing is complete, she will ask them to compare the two pictures and see that their anger may be masking their feelings of sadness, loneliness, and disappointment. As patients begin to recognize their true feelings, they develop better control of their behavior.

To reach their patients, creative arts therapists can use a variety of mediums, including visual art, music, dance, drama, or poetry or other kinds of creative writing. Creative arts therapists usually specialize in a specific medium, becoming a music therapist, drama therapist, dance therapist, art therapist, or poetry therapist. "In my groups we use poetry and creative writing," Fish explains. "We do all kinds of things to get at what is going on at an unconscious level."

Music therapists use musical lessons and activities to improve a patient's self-confidence and self-awareness, to relieve states of depression, and to improve physical dexterity. For example, a music therapist treating a patient with Alzheimer's might play songs from the patient's past in order to stimulate long- and short-term memory, soothe feelings of agitation, and increase a sense of reality.

Art therapists use art in much the same manner. The art therapist may encourage and teach patients to express their thoughts, feelings, and anxieties via sketching, drawing, painting, or sculpting. Art therapy is especially helpful in revealing patterns of domestic abuse in families. Children involved in such a situation may depict scenes of family life with violent details or portray a certain family member as especially frightening or threatening.

Dance/movement therapists develop and conduct dance/movement sessions to help improve the physical, mental, and emotional health of their patients. Dance and movement therapy is also used as a way of assessing a patient's progress toward reaching therapeutic goals.

There are other types of creative arts therapists as well. *Drama therapists* use role-playing, pantomime (the telling of a story by the use of expressive body or facial movements), puppetry, improvisation, and original scripted dramatization to evaluate and treat patients. *Poetry therapists* and *bibliotherapists*, use the written and spoken word to treat patients.

REQUIREMENTS

High School

To become a creative arts therapist, you will need a bachelor's degree, so take a college preparatory curriculum while in high school. You should become as proficient as possible with the methods and tools related to the type of creative arts therapy you wish to pursue. When therapists work with patients they must be able to concentrate completely on the patient rather than on learning how to use tools or techniques. For example, if you want to become involved in music therapy, you need to be familiar with musical instruments as well as music theory. A good starting point for a music therapist is to study piano or guitar.

In addition to courses such as drama, art, music, and English, you should consider taking an introductory class in psychology. Also, a communication class will give you an understanding of the various ways people communicate, both verbally and nonverbally.

Postsecondary Training

To become a creative arts therapist you must earn at least a bachelor's degree, usually in the area in which you wish to specialize. For example, those studying to be art therapists typically have undergraduate degrees in studio art, art education, or psychology with a strong emphasis on art courses as well.

In most cases, however, you will also need a graduate degree before you can gain certification as a professional or advance in your chosen field. Requirements for admission to graduate schools vary by program, so you would be wise to contact the graduate programs you are interested in to find out about their admissions policies. For some fields you may be required to submit a portfolio of your work along with the written application. Professional organizations can be a good source of information regarding high-quality programs. For example, both the American Art Therapy Association and the American Music Therapy Association provide lists of schools that meet their standards for approval. (Contact information for both associations are listed at the end of this article.)

In graduate school, your study of psychology and the arts field you are interested in will be in-depth. Classes for someone seeking a master's in art therapy, for example, may include group psychotherapy, foundation of creativity theory, assessment and treatment planning, and art therapy presentation. In addition to classroom study you will also complete an internship or supervised practicum (that is, work with clients). Depending on your program, you may also need to write a thesis or present a final artistic project before receiving your degree.

Certification or Licensing

Typically, the nationally recognized association or certification board specific to your field of choice offers registration and certification. For example, the Art Therapy Credentials Board (ATCB) offers registration and certification to art therapists, and the American Dance Therapy Association offers registration to dance therapists. In general, requirements for registration include completing an approved therapy program and having a certain amount of experience working with clients. Requirements for higher levels of registration or certification generally involve having additional work experience and passing a written exam.

For a specific example, consider the certification process for an art therapist: an art therapist may receive the designation art therapist registered from the ATCB after completing a graduate program and having some experience working with clients. The next level, then, is to become an art therapist registered-board certified by passing a written exam. To retain certification status, therapists must complete a certain amount of continuing education.

Many registered creative arts therapists also hold additional licenses in other fields, such as social work, education, mental health, or marriage and family therapy. In some states, creative arts therapists need licensing depending on their place of work. For specific information on licensing in your field, you will need to check with your state's licensing board. Creative arts therapists are also often members of other professional associations, including the American Psychological Association, the American Association for Marriage and Family Therapy, and the American Counseling Association.

Other Requirements

To succeed in this line of work, you should have a strong desire to help others seek positive change in their lives. All types of creative arts therapists must be able to work well with other people—both patients and other health professionals—in the development and implementation of therapy programs. You must have the patience and the stamina to teach and practice therapy with patients for whom progress is often very slow because of their various physical and emotional disorders. A therapist must always keep in mind that even a tiny amount of progress might be extremely significant for some patients and their families. A good sense of humor is also a valuable trait.

EXPLORING

There are many ways to explore the possibility of a career as a creative arts therapist. Visit the websites of professional associations for information on therapy careers. Talk with people working in the creative arts therapy field and perhaps arrange to observe a creative arts therapy session. Look for part-time or summer jobs or volunteer at a hospital, clinic, nursing home, or any of a number of health care facilities.

A summer job as an aide at a camp for disabled children, for example, may help provide insight into the nature of creative arts therapy, including both its rewards and demands. Such experience can be very valuable in deciding if you are suited to the inherent frustrations of a therapy career.

EMPLOYERS

Creative arts therapists usually work as members of an interdisciplinary health care team that may include physicians, nurses, social workers, psychiatrists, and psychologists. Although often employed

Potential Employers

- Adult Day Treatment Centers
- Community Mental Health Centers
- Community Residences and Halfway Houses
- Correctional and Forensic Facilities
- Disaster Relief Centers
- Drug and Alcohol Programs
- Early Intervention Programs
- General Hospitals
- Home Health Agencies
- Hospices
- Neonatal Nurseries
- Nursing Homes
- Outpatient Clinics
- Psychiatric Units and Hospitals
- Rehabilitative Facilities
- Schools
- Senior Centers
- Wellness Centers

Source: National Coalition of Arts Therapies Associations

in hospitals, therapists also work in rehabilitation centers, nursing homes, day treatment facilities, shelters for battered women, pain and stress management clinics, substance abuse programs, hospices, and correctional facilities. Others maintain their own private practices. Many creative arts therapists work with children in grammar and high schools, either as therapists or art teachers. Some arts therapists teach or conduct research in the creative arts at colleges and universities.

STARTING OUT

After earning a bachelor's degree in a particular field, you should complete your certification, which may include an internship or assistantship. Unpaid training internships often can lead to a first job in the field. Graduates can use the career services office at their college or university to help them find positions in the creative arts therapy field. Many professional associations also compile lists of job openings to assist their members.

Creative arts therapists who are new to the field might consider doing volunteer work at a nonprofit community organization, correctional facility, or neighborhood association to gain some practical experience. Therapists who want to start their own practice can host group therapy sessions in their homes. Creative arts therapists may also wish to associate with other members of the alternative health care field in order to gain experience and build a client base.

ADVANCEMENT

With more experience, therapists can move into supervisory, administrative, and teaching positions. Often, the supervision of interns can resemble a therapy session. The interns will discuss their feelings and ask questions they may have regarding their work with clients. How did they handle their clients? What were the reactions to what their clients said or did? What could they be doing to help more? The supervising therapist helps the interns become competent creative arts therapists.

Many therapists have represented the profession internationally. Barbara Fish was invited to present her paper, "Art Therapy with Children and Adolescents," at the University of Helsinki. Additionally, Fish spoke in Finland at a three-day workshop exploring the use and effectiveness of arts therapy with children and adolescents. Raising the public and professional awareness of creative arts therapy is an important concern for many therapists.

EARNINGS

A therapist's annual salary depends on experience, level of training, and education. Working on a hospital staff or being self-employed also affects annual income. According to the American Art Therapy Association (AATA), entry-level art therapists earn annual salaries of approximately $28,000. Median annual salaries are $42,000, and the AATA reports that top earnings for salaried administrators ranged from $50,000 and $100,000 annually. Those who have Ph.D.'s and are licensed for private practice can earn between $75 and $150 per hour, according to the AATA; however, professional expenses such as insurance and office rental must be paid by those in private practice.

The American Music Therapy Association reported average annual salaries for music therapists as $34,893 in 2000. Salaries varied from that average by region, most by less than $2,000 a year, with the highest average salaries reported in the New England states at $41,600. Salaries reported by its members ranged from $15,000 to $81,000. The average annual earnings for music therapists with more than 20 years of professional experience was $43,306 in 2000.

Benefits depend on the employer but generally include paid vacation time, health insurance, and paid sick days. Those who are in private practice must provide their own benefits.

WORK ENVIRONMENT

Most creative arts therapists work a typical 40-hour, five-day workweek; at times, however, they may have to work extra hours. The number of patients under a therapist's care depends on the specific employment setting. Although many therapists work in hospitals, they may also be employed in such facilities as clinics, rehabilitation centers, children's homes, schools, and nursing homes. Some therapists maintain service contracts with several facilities. For instance, a therapist might work two days a week at a hospital, one day at a nursing home, and the rest of the week at a rehabilitation center.

Most buildings are pleasant, comfortable, and clean places in which to work. Experienced creative arts therapists might choose to be self-employed, working with patients in their own studios. In such a case, the therapist might work more irregular hours to accommodate patient schedules. Other therapists might maintain a combination of service contract work with one or more facilities in addition to a private caseload of clients referred to them by other health care professionals. Whether therapists work on service contracts with various facilities or maintain private practices, they must deal with all of the business and administrative details and worries that go along with being self-employed.

OUTLOOK

The American Art Therapy Association notes that this is a growing field. Demand for new therapists is created as medical professionals and the general public become aware of the benefits gained through art therapies. Although enrollment in college therapy programs is increasing, new graduates are usually able to find jobs. In cases where an individual is unable to find a full-time position, a therapist might obtain service contracts for part-time work at several facilities.

Job openings in facilities such as nursing homes should continue to increase as the elderly population grows over the next few decades. Advances in medical technology and the recent practice of early discharge from hospitals should also create new opportunities in managed care facilities, chronic pain clinics, and cancer care facilities. The demand for therapists of all types should continue to increase as more people become aware of the need to help disabled patients in creative ways. Some drama therapists and psychodramatists are also finding employment opportunities outside of the usual health care field. Such therapists might conduct therapy sessions at corporate sites to enhance the personal effectiveness and growth of employees.

FOR MORE INFORMATION

For more detailed information about your field of interest, contact the following organizations:

American Art Therapy Association
5999 Stevenson Avenue
Alexandria, VA 22304
Tel: 888-290-0878
Email: info@arttherapy.org
http://www.arttherapy.org

American Dance Therapy Association
2000 Century Plaza, Suite 108
10632 Little Patuxent Parkway
Columbia, MD 21044
Tel: 410-997-4040
Email: info@adta.org
http://www.adta.org

American Music Therapy Association
8455 Colesville Road, Suite 1000
Silver Spring, MD 20910
Tel: 301-589-3300
Email: info@musictherapy.org
http://www.musictherapy.org

American Society of Group Psychotherapy and Psychodrama
301 North Harrison Street, Suite 508
Princeton, NJ 08540
Tel: 609-452-1339
Email: asgpp@asgpp.org
http://www.asgpp.org

National Association for Drama Therapy
15 Post Side Lane
Pittsford, NY 14534
Tel: 585-381-5618
Email: answers@nadt.org
http://www.nadt.org

National Association for Poetry Therapy
525 SW 5th Street, Suite A
Des Moines, Iowa 50309-4501
Tel: 866-844-NAPT
Email: info@poetrytherapy.org
http://www.poetrytherapy.org

For an overview of the various types of art therapy, visit the NCATA website.
National Coalition of Arts Therapies Associations (NCATA)
c/o AMTA
8455 Colesville Road, Suite 1000
Silver Spring, MD 20910
Tel: 201-224-9146
http://www.nccata.org

Elementary School Teachers

OVERVIEW

Elementary school teachers instruct students from the first through sixth or eighth grades. They develop teaching outlines and lesson plans, give lectures, facilitate discussions and activities, keep class attendance records, assign homework, and evaluate student progress. Most teachers work with one group of children throughout the day, teaching several subjects and supervising such activities as lunch and recess. More than 1.5 million elementary school teachers are employed in the United States.

HISTORY

The history of elementary education can be traced back to about 100 B.C., when the people of Judah established schools for young children as part of their religious training.

In the early days of Western elementary education, the teacher only had to have completed elementary school to be considered qualified to teach. There was little incentive for an elementary school teacher to seek further education. School terms were generally short (about six months) and buildings were often cramped and poorly heated. Many elementary schools combined the entire eight grades into one room, teaching the same course of study for all ages. In these earliest schools, teachers were not well paid and had little status or recognition in the community.

When people began to realize that teachers should be better educated, schools designed to train teachers, called normal schools, were established. The first normal school was private and opened in Concord, Vermont, in 1823. The first state-supported normal school was established in Lexington, Massachusetts, in 1839. By 1900, nearly every state had at least one state-supported normal school.

The forerunner of the present-day college or school of education in large universities was the normal department established at Indiana University in 1852. Normal schools have since then given way to teachers' colleges. Today almost every university in the country has a school or college of education.

THE JOB

Elementary school teachers teach grades one through six or eight (depending on the school). In smaller schools, grades may be combined. There are still a few one-room, one-teacher elementary schools in remote rural areas. However, in most cases, teachers instruct approximately 20 to 30 children of the same grade. They teach a variety of subjects in the prescribed course of study, including language, science, mathematics, and social studies. In the classroom, teachers use various methods to educate their students, such as reading to them, assigning group projects, and showing films for discussion. Teachers also use educational games to help their pupils remember their lessons.

In the first and second grades, elementary school teachers cover the basic skills: reading, writing, counting, and telling time. With older students, teachers instruct history, geography, math, English, and handwriting. To capture attention and teach new concepts, they use arts and crafts projects, workbooks, music, and other interactive activities. In the upper grades, teachers assign written and oral reports and involve students in projects and competitions such as spelling bees, science fairs, and math contests. Although they are usually required to follow a curriculum designed by state or local administrators, teachers study new learning methods to incorporate into the classroom, such as using computers to surf the Internet.

"I utilize many different, some unorthodox, teaching tools," says Andrea LoCastro, a sixth-grade teacher in Clayton, New Jersey. "I have a lunchtime chess club. Students give up their recess to listen to classical music and play, or learn to play, chess." She has also found that role-playing activities keep her students interested in the various subjects. "We are studying ancient Greece," she says, "and I currently have my students writing persuasive essays as either part of Odysseus' legal team or the Cyclops' legal team. I intend to culminate the activity with a mock trial, Athenian style."

To create unique exercises and activities such as those LoCastro uses, teachers need to devote a fair amount of time to preparation outside of the classroom. They prepare daily lesson plans and assignments, grade papers and tests, and keep a record of each student's progress. Other responsibilities include communicating with parents through written reports and scheduled meetings, keeping their classroom orderly, and decorating desks and bulletin boards to keep the learning environment visually stimulating.

Elementary school teachers may also teach music, art, and physical education, but these areas are often covered by specialized teachers. *Art teachers* are responsible for developing art projects, procuring supplies, and helping students develop drawing, painting, sculpture, mural design, ceramics, and other artistic abilities. Some art teachers also teach students about the history of art and lead field trips to local museums. *Music teachers* teach music appreciation and history. They direct organized student groups such as choruses, bands, or orchestras, or guide music classes by accompanying them in singing songs or playing instruments. Often, music teachers are responsible for organizing school pageants, musicals, and plays. *Physical education teachers* help students develop physical skills such as coordination, strength, and stamina and social skills such as self-confidence and good sportsmanship. Physical education teachers often serve as sports coaches and may be responsible for organizing field days and intramural activities.

When working with elementary-aged children, teachers need to instruct social skills along with general school subjects. They serve as disciplinarians, establishing and enforcing rules of conduct to help students learn right from wrong. To keep the classroom manageable, teachers maintain a system of rewards and punishments to encourage students to behave, stay interested, and participate. In cases of classroom disputes, teachers must also be mediators, teaching their pupils to peacefully work through arguments.

Recent developments in school curricula have led to new teaching arrangements and methods. In some schools, one or more teachers work with students within a small age range instead of with particular grades. Other schools are adopting bilingual education, where students are instructed throughout the day in two languages by either a *bilingual teacher* or two separate teachers.

Many teachers find it rewarding to witness students develop and hone new skills and adopt an appreciation for learning. In fact, many teachers inspire their own students to later join the teaching profession themselves. "Teaching is not just a career," says LoCastro, "It is a commitment—a commitment to the 20-plus children that walk

An elementary school
educator teaches
reading comprehension
skills to two students.
(Jim Whitmer
Photography)

into your classroom door each September eager for enlightenment
and fun."

REQUIREMENTS

High School

Follow your school's college preparatory program and take advanced
courses in English, mathematics, science, history, and government to
prepare for an education degree. Art, music, physical education, and
extracurricular activities will contribute to a broad base of knowledge necessary to teach a variety of subjects. Composition, journal-
ism, and communications classes are also important for developing
your writing and speaking skills.

Postsecondary Training

All 50 states and the District of Columbia require public elementary
education teachers to have a bachelor's degree in either education or in
the subject they plan to teach. Prospective teachers must also complete
an approved training program. In the United States, there are more
than 500 accredited teacher education programs, which combine subject and educational classes with work experience in the classroom.

   Though programs vary by state, courses cover how to instruct
language arts, mathematics, physical science, social science, art, and

music. Additionally, prospective teachers must take educational training courses, such as philosophy of education, child psychology, and learning methods. To gain experience in the classroom, student teachers are placed in a school to work with a full-time teacher. During this training period, student teachers observe the ways in which lessons are presented and the classroom is managed, learn how to keep records of attendance and grades, and gain experience in handling the class, both under supervision and alone.

Some states require prospective teachers to have master's degrees in education and specialized technology training to keep them familiar with more modern teaching methods using computers and the Internet.

Certification or Licensing
Public school teachers must be licensed under regulations established by the state in which they are teaching. If moving, teachers have to comply with any other regulations in their new state to be able to teach, though many states have reciprocity agreements that make it easier for teachers to change locations.

Licensure examinations test prospective teachers for competency in basic subjects such as mathematics, reading, writing, teaching, and other subject matter proficiency. In addition, many states are moving towards a performance-based evaluation for licensing. In this case, after passing the teaching examination, prospective teachers are given provisional licenses. Only after proving themselves capable in the classroom are they eligible for a full license.

Another growing trend spurred by recent teacher shortages is alternative licensure arrangements. For those who have a bachelor's degree but lack formal education courses and training in the classroom, states can issue a provisional license. These workers immediately begin teaching under the supervision of a licensed educator for one to two years and take education classes outside of their working hours. Once they have completed the required coursework and gained experience in the classroom, they are granted a full license. This flexible licensing arrangement has helped to bring additional teachers into school systems needing instructors.

Other Requirements
Many consider the desire to teach a calling. This calling is based on a love of children and a dedication to their welfare. If you want to become a teacher, you must respect children as individuals, with personalities, strengths, and weaknesses of their own. You must also be patient and self-disciplined to manage a large group independently.

Teachers make a powerful impression on children, so they need to serve as good role models. "Treat students with kindness and understanding, rules and consequences," LoCastro suggests. "Be nice, yet strict. They'll love you for it."

EXPLORING

To explore the teaching career, look for leadership opportunities that involve working with children. You might find summer work as a counselor in a summer camp, as a leader of a scout troop, or as an assistant in a public park or community center. Look for opportunities to tutor younger students or coach children's athletic teams. Local community theaters may need directors and assistants for summer children's productions. Day care centers often hire high school students for late afternoon and weekend work.

EMPLOYERS

There are more than 1.5 million elementary school teachers employed in the United States. Teachers are needed at public and private institutions, including parochial schools and Montessori schools, which focus more on the child's own initiatives. Teachers are also needed in day care centers that offer full-day elementary programs and charter schools, which are smaller, deregulated schools that receive public funding. Although rural areas maintain schools, more teaching positions are available in urban or suburban areas.

STARTING OUT

After obtaining a college degree, finishing the student teaching program, and becoming certified, prospective teachers have many avenues for finding a job. College placement offices and state departments of education maintain listings of job openings. Many local schools advertise teaching positions in newspapers. Another option is directly contacting the administration in the schools in which you'd like to work. While looking for a full-time position, you can work as a substitute teacher. In more urban areas with many schools, you may be able to find full-time substitute work.

ADVANCEMENT

As teachers acquire experience or additional education, they can expect higher wages and more responsibilities. Teachers with leadership skills and an interest in administrative work may advance to serve as principals or supervisors, though the number of these positions is limited and competition is fierce. Others may advance to work as *senior* or *mentor teachers* who assist less experienced staff. Another move may be into higher education, teaching education classes at a college or university. For most of these positions, additional education is required.

Other common career transitions are into related fields. With additional preparation, teachers can become librarians, reading specialists, or counselors.

"I intend to continue teaching as my career," says Andrea LoCastro. "I am not at all interested in moving up to administration. I will, however, pursue a master's in teaching after receiving tenure."

EARNINGS

According to the U.S. Department of Labor, the median annual salary for elementary school teachers was $43,660 in 2004. The lowest 10 percent earned $29,370; the highest 10 percent earned $68,930 or more. The average salary for beginning teachers with a bachelor's degree was $31,704 in 2004, according to the American Federation of Teachers. Private school teachers generally earn less than public school teachers.

Teachers often supplement their earnings through teaching summer classes, coaching sports, sponsoring a club, or other extracurricular work. More than half of all teachers belong to unions such as the American Federation of Teachers or the National Education Association. These unions bargain with schools over contract conditions such as wages, hours, and benefits. Depending on the state, teachers usually receive a retirement plan, sick leave, and health and life insurance. Some systems grant teachers sabbatical leave.

WORK ENVIRONMENT

Most teachers are contracted to work 10 months out of the year, with a two-month vacation during the summer. During their summer break, many continue their education to renew or upgrade their teaching licenses and earn higher salaries. Teachers in schools that operate year-round work eight-week sessions with one-week breaks in between and a five-week vacation in the winter.

Teachers work in generally pleasant conditions, although some older schools may have poor heating or electrical systems. The work can seem confining, requiring them to remain in the classroom throughout most of the day. Although the job is not overly strenuous, dealing with busy children all day can be tiring and trying. Teachers must stand for many hours each day, do a lot of talking, show energy and enthusiasm, and handle any discipline problems. But, according to Andrea LoCastro, problems with students are usually overshadowed by their successes. "Just knowing a child is learning something because of you is the most rewarding feeling, especially when you and the child have struggled together to understand it."

OUTLOOK

According to the *Occupational Outlook Handbook,* employment opportunities for teachers (grades K–12) are expected to grow as fast as the average for all occupations through 2012. The need to replace retiring teachers will provide many opportunities nationwide.

The demand for teachers varies widely depending on geographic area. Inner-city schools characterized by poor working conditions and low salaries often suffer a shortage of teachers. In addition, more opportunities exist for those who specialize in a subject in which it is harder to attract qualified teachers, such as mathematics, science, or foreign languages.

The National Education Association believes it will be a difficult challenge to hire enough new teachers to meet rising enrollments and replace the large number of retiring teachers, primarily because of low teacher salaries. Approximately 2.4 million teachers will be needed to fill classrooms in the next decade. Higher salaries along with other necessary changes, such as smaller classroom sizes and safer schools, will be necessary to attract new teachers and retain experienced ones. Other challenges for the profession involve attracting more men into teaching. The percentage of male teachers continues to decline.

In order to improve education, drastic changes are being considered by some districts. Some private companies are managing public schools in the hope of providing better facilities, faculty, and equipment. Teacher organizations are concerned about taking school management away from communities and turning it over to remote corporate headquarters.

Charter schools and voucher programs are two other controversial alternatives to traditional public education. Publicly funded charter schools are not guided by the rules and regulations of traditional public schools. Some view these schools as places of innovation and improved educational methods; others see them as ill-equipped and unfairly funded with money that could better benefit local school districts. Vouchers, which exist only in a few cities, use public tax dollars to allow students to attend private schools. In theory, the vouchers allow for more choices in education for poor and minority students. Teacher organizations see some danger in giving public funds to unregulated private schools and fear that voucher programs will degrade the quality of public schools by reducing their funding.

FOR MORE INFORMATION

For information about careers, education, and union membership, contact the following organizations:

American Federation of Teachers
555 New Jersey Avenue, NW
Washington, DC 20001
Tel: 202-879-4400
Email: online@aft.org
http://www.aft.org

National Council for Accreditation of Teacher Education
2010 Massachusetts Avenue, NW, Suite 500
Washington, DC 20036-1023
Tel: 202-466-7496
Email: ncate@ncate.org
http://www.ncate.org

National Education Association
1201 16th Street, NW
Washington, DC 20036-3290
Tel: 202-833-4000
http://www.nea.org

Guidance Counselors

OVERVIEW

Guidance counselors provide a planned program of guidance services for all students, principally in junior and senior high schools. In addition to helping students plan for college and careers, guidance counselors listen to students' problems, advise students, and help them develop coping skills and learn to become good problem-solvers and decision-makers on their own.

Although guidance counselors often meet with students individually, they may also work with groups, organizing several students for special meetings to address a problem or issue that the students have in common. There are approximately 228,000 educational, vocational, and school counselors employed in the United States.

HISTORY

Counseling in secondary schools, as a comprehensive guidance service, is an outgrowth of the earlier program of vocational guidance in schools. Such programs were slowly adopted by school systems through the 1920s—Boston and New York being among the first—but during the Depression years, school budgets were at a low point and the vocational guidance movement came to a standstill.

After World War II, guidance services began to show signs of growth. Many factors contributed to the sudden spurt. There was a great migration from rural to urban living, and city schools became overcrowded. Students lost their individual identity in the crowds of fellow students. More courses were being offered in more schools, and choices were difficult to make. Changes in careers because of

A guidance counselor discusses college planning with a high school student. *(Jim Whitmer Photography)*

technological developments made it difficult for parents to help their children with wise career choices. Living standards improved, and more parents, who themselves had not gone to college, planned a college education for their children. In the years following World War II, school guidance programs grew both in number and in expanded fields. Many colleges and universities initiated training programs for guidance counselors, and licensure standards for counselors were established or upgraded. The U.S. Office of Education embarked upon an ambitious leadership program for guidance services as the need for professionals in the field increased.

THE JOB

Guidance counselors work in a school setting to provide a planned program of guidance services for the benefit of all students enrolled in the school. The guidance program is not one single plan, but is the combination of many related activities. It has several aims, but its most important one is to help each student in the process of growth toward maturity. The guidance program is designed to help students achieve independence.

All guidance programs are unique. Each one is built especially for the school in which it functions. Guidance counselors confer with parents, with professional personnel such as school psychologists, social workers, and health officers, and with other faculty and staff members to assure a totally effective school program. They meet with students on an appointment, walk-in, or teacher-referral basis to talk about students' personal problems or concerns; to review academic, attendance, or conduct records; or to discuss anything else that may be an issue to the students, faculty, or parents.

Jim Buist is a middle school counselor. "I work with about 800 young people during a highly charged transitional period of their lives," he says. "My primary role as a school counselor is to aid these young people in a successful educational process." This involves a number of tasks: scheduling (matching students with teachers and courses); testing (to monitor progress); and counseling (to guide young people through the troubles of adolescence).

Students seek out Buist's advice on such subjects as family issues, peer pressure, alcohol/drug problems, the development of romantic relationships, and illness and death. "Besides working with the students themselves," Buist says, "I have the obligation and opportunity to work with other professionals as teams or supports, as well as with parents who are often looking for the manual that was supposed to come with their children."

In addition to dealing directly with students, guidance counselors collect and organize materials for students to read about such topics as peer-pressure, self-esteem, occupations, and post–high school educational opportunities. They conduct group guidance meetings in which topics of special concern or interest to the age group involved are discussed. For example, they may direct an orientation program for students new to the school. In addition, they organize, administer, score, and interpret the school's standardized testing program.

Guidance counselors assist students in choosing their courses of studies, developing more effective study habits, and making tentative choices regarding goals for the future. They help students in selecting the post–high school training that will best meet their educational and vocational needs. They also assist students in applying for admission to colleges or vocational schools, help locate scholarships, and write reference letters to college admissions officers or prospective employers.

Guidance counselors plan, organize, and conduct events such as career days and college days. They may conduct follow-up studies of students who have left school or graduated, requesting their help in evaluating the curriculum in the light of their post–high school work experiences.

Guidance counselors also conduct in-service education courses for other faculty members or speak at meetings of interested members of the community. They refer students with problems that are beyond the scope of school counseling to such community resources as social welfare agencies, child guidance clinics, health departments, or other services.

REQUIREMENTS

High School

Enroll in a college preparatory curriculum to prepare for the college degrees required of guidance counselors. You should take courses in humanities, social studies, and psychology. Courses in mathematics are important, because mathematical and statistical theory underlie much of the standardized testing program. You should take English and speech courses because both written and spoken communication with students, parents, and administrators are key components to this occupation.

Postsecondary Training

The basic requirement for a school counselor in many states is a bachelor's degree and certain stipulated courses at the graduate level. Most guidance counselors earn a master's degree in counseling in order to be eligible for professional certification and to meet the licensing requirements of many states. As an undergraduate, you'll probably major in education so that you'll have the course work necessary for teacher certification. The American Counseling Association (ACA) and the American School Counselor Association provide information to students when selecting graduate programs in counselor education.

To get accepted into a graduate program, you'll have to have a bachelor's degree and possibly a teaching certificate and a few years teaching experience. These programs usually require at least two years of additional study, as well as an internship. Course subjects include career development, group counseling, substance abuse counseling, art therapy, and grief and loss counseling.

Certification or Licensing

You must be certified by your state to work as a counselor; the requirements for certification vary from state to state. Most state licensure standards require that counselors have teaching experience. This experience may be as short as one year or as long as two to three years. Some states also require that counselors have work experience outside of the teaching field.

The National Board for Certified Counselors (NBCC) offers the national certified counselor (NCC) designation as well as the national certified school counselor (NCSC) designation. Requirements vary for each certification; contact the NBCC for more information.

Other Requirements

Your most important asset will be your ability to relate easily and well to others. To achieve a sound relationship with other adults and with children, you must have a sincere interest in other people and their welfare. You must be able to relate to all kinds of people and situations, and to be sensitive to issues of race, religion, sexual orientation, and disability. Jim Buist lists empathy, patience, and listening skills among the personal qualities that make a good counselor. He emphasizes that counselors should have some teaching experience in their background. Without that experience, Buist says, "you'll be missing the experience that you'll need day in and day out. It would be difficult, if not impossible, to learn these skills 'on the job.'"

EXPLORING

Your best resource for information about work as a guidance counselor is right in your own high school. Ask your school's counselor how he or she got started in the career, and about the nature of the job. You may even be allowed to assist your counselor with a variety of projects like career days or college recruitment. With your counselor's help, you can identify some of the particular issues affecting your fellow students and come up with ways to address the issues with special projects. You can also get a sense of a counselor's job by working on the school newspaper. As a reporter, you'll have the opportunity to interview students, get to know their concerns, and write editorials about these issues.

The ACA publishes a great deal of information about the field of professional guidance. The ACA website (http://www.counseling.org) features many articles about counseling; ACA also produces a monthly publication called *Counseling Today*. An electronic version, called *CTOnline*, is available at the website.

EMPLOYERS

Approximately 228,000 educational, vocational, and school counselors are employed in the United States. Counselors are employed in elementary, middle, and high schools all across the country. They work in both public and private schools. Though counselors are considered important to a school system, not every school has its own counselor on staff. Some counselors have offices in more than one school; for example, they may work for both a middle school and a high school, or they may work for other schools in the district.

STARTING OUT

While some students do enroll in master's programs right after finishing their undergraduate programs, most experts advise that you get at least a few years of teaching experience under your belt before you pursue a master's degree in counselor education. Some people work for several years as teachers before considering a degree in school counseling. College professors and advisers should be able to direct you to sources of counseling positions. Some state boards of education maintain job lines, as do many public school districts. These jobs are also advertised in the newspaper.

The ACA lists job openings across the country in its publication *Counseling Today,* and on its website. The American School Counselor Association offers professional development programs to help members expand skills, knowledge, and networking opportunities.

ADVANCEMENT

Schools with more than one counselor on the staff offer the opportunity for staff members to advance to *school guidance director.* The title may be misleading, however, as one does not usually "direct" the program; rather, one coordinates it. The school principal is usually the actual director of the program. Most advancement within the guidance counselor position will be in the form of wage increases.

Some counselors with many years of experience may be appointed as *guidance coordinator* or *director* for a city or county school system. Their duties usually include program development.

For the most part, counselors are promoted to positions outside of counseling itself, such as to administration or supervisory jobs. Some counselors obtain advanced degrees and become college or university teachers. Jim Buist has had many opportunities to move into administrative positions, but has turned them down. "I know I would miss the contact with the students, parents, and teachers," he says.

EARNINGS

Wages for guidance counselors vary by region of the country, school and district size, and age of the students. Larger districts typically offer higher salaries, and counselors working with high school students tend to earn more than counselors for younger grades. According to the U.S. Department of Labor, the median salary for educational, vocational, and school counselors was $46,160 in 2004. Earnings in 2004 ranged from less than $26,610 to $72,970 or more.

Because guidance counselors work on an academic calendar, they typically get a good amount of vacation time, especially in the summer. Some counselors use this time to take additional university courses. Counselors receive the benefits and pension plans provided by the school or district that employs them.

WORK ENVIRONMENT

Most guidance counselors have a private office in which to talk with students, parents, and faculty members. But they also work in other parts of the school, leading presentations, coordinating events, and speaking to classes of students. Counselors find it rewarding to help students through their problems, and to help them plan for their futures, but they also have the stress of guiding young people through difficult times. "This is an age where a counselor/teacher can make a difference," Jim Buist says.

Guidance counselors usually work more than 40 hours a week, spending a part of each day in conferences and meetings. They often arrive at school earlier than do many other staff members and may return to the school in the evening to talk with parents who are unable to come to the school during working hours.

OUTLOOK

The U.S. Department of Labor predicts that the employment of school counselors will increase about as fast as the average for all other occupations through 2012. Increasing enrollments at the secondary level and state legislation requiring counselors at the elementary school level will ensure continued demand for workers in this field.

Though violence in the schools has been decreasing, some students are afraid to go to school. This fear may be a result of the rash of shootings and gang-related warfare that plagued some schools in the late 1990s. The federal government has called for more counselors in the schools to help address issues of violence and other dangers, such as drug use. The government, along with counseling professionals, is also working to remove the stigma of mental illness and to encourage more children and families to seek help from school counselors. To keep schools safe, guidance counselors may be more actively involved in instituting and maintaining discipline policies.

Technology will continue to assist counselors in their jobs. With Internet access in the libraries, counselors can easily direct students to specific career information, scholarship applications, and college websites. School counselors may also follow the lead of Internet counselors and offer guidance online; students seeking anonymity can request information and advice from their counselors through email and other online services.

FOR MORE INFORMATION

For information about counseling careers and graduate school programs, contact
American Counseling Association
5999 Stevenson Avenue
Alexandria, VA 22304
Tel: 800-347-6647
http://www.counseling.org

For information about careers, accredited counseling programs, and state certification requirements, contact
American School Counselor Association
1101 King Street, Suite 625
Alexandria, VA 22314
Tel: 703-683-2722
Email: asca@schoolcounselor.org
http://www.schoolcounselor.org

For information about college admission counseling and a list of related publications, contact
National Association for College Admission Counseling
1631 Prince Street
Alexandria, VA 22314-2818
Tel: 703-836-2222
http://www.nacacnet.org

For information on certification, contact
National Board for Certified Counselors
3 Terrace Way, Suite D
Greensboro, NC 27403-3660

Tel: 336-547-0607
Email: nbcc@nbcc.org
http://www.nbcc.org

INTERVIEW

Bethanne Schlee is currently pursuing a Ph.D. in human sciences with an emphasis in child development and family relations at Florida State University in Tallahassee, Florida. She was kind enough to discuss her educational career with the editors of Careers in Focus: Child Care.

Q. What are the most challenging aspects of being a Ph.D. student?

A. The most challenging part of being a Ph.D. student would be time management. As of right now, I teach a class of 120 undergraduates; serve as a research associate for a team of faculty, the secretary of the College of Human Sciences Advisory Council, and the child development representative for the Graduate Student Advisory Council; and am trying to write my dissertation. Along with all of the activities that I am involved with, as a doctoral student, I am also expected to attend college functions, present at national conferences, and be publishing studies. There is not much free time, so it helps that I do not live in the same state as my family, as I know I would not get as much school work done as I would like if I lived near them.

Q. Tell us about your dissertation.

A. My dissertation focuses on looking at teachers' perceptions of their role in the development of early literacy skills in preschool children. I am very interested in knowing what teachers believe is their job and what they believe should be taught at home. With 72 percent of young children in child care, there is a need to see what teachers believe and the role they play with the children in their classrooms.

Q. What career do you plan to pursue once you complete your degree?

A. I would love to teach and do research at the university level. I love teaching child development and family relations as well as being involved with a variety of research projects. I would also love to do some advocacy work in the realm of child care as well.

Nannies

OVERVIEW

Nannies, also known as *au pairs,* are caregivers who care for children in the parents' homes. The children usually range in age from infant to 11 years old. The nanny's responsibilities may include supervising the nursery, organizing play activities, taking the children to appointments or classes, and keeping the children's quarters clean and intact. They may be responsible for supervising the child part of the day or the entire day.

In a large and growing percentage of American families, both parents hold full-time jobs and require full-time child care, which has resulted in increased employment opportunities for nannies. In many other families, parents are opting for part-time work or running businesses out of their homes. Although this allows the parents to be with their children more than if they worked a traditional job, the unpredictability of children's needs makes a nanny's help welcome. A growing segment of parents prefer that their children be cared for at home as opposed to taking them to day care or a babysitter. Thus, the nanny has become a viable and often satisfactory solution.

QUICK FACTS

School Subjects
Family and consumer science
Psychology

Personal Skills
Communication/ideas
Helping/teaching

Work Environment
Primarily indoors
Primarily one location

Minimum Education Level
High school diploma

Salary Range
$12,330 to $20,750 to $26,100+

Certification or Licensing
Voluntary

Outlook
About as fast as the average

DOT
301

GOE
12.03.03

NOC
6474

O*NET-SOC
39-9011.00

HISTORY

Nannies have been a staple of European staffs for hundreds of years, often epitomizing the upper-class British childhood. They have captured our imaginations and have been the basis for fictional characters ranging from Jane Eyre to Mary Poppins. In the United States, nannies or nursemaids have worked in the homes of the very wealthy for centuries. Only quite recently, however, has the role of the nanny entered into the lives of the middle class.

A nanny plays with two young children. *(Jim Whitmer Photography)*

Because of the steadily increasing demand for highly skilled, reliable, private child care, nannies have gained such popularity that schools have sprung up across the country to train and place them. However, the vast majority of nannies come from overseas. Young women and men from the West Indies, the Philippines, Ireland, South Central America, and other regions often emigrate to the United States to become nannies because of the poor economic conditions in their own countries. These nannies are often taken advantage of by the people they work for. They may be paid next to nothing, and be expected to be completely at the disposal of the family, even at a moment's notice, and they usually receive no health insurance or other benefits. Unfortunately, they put up with this sort of treatment mainly because they are afraid to lose the income, a large part of which they often send home to relatives in their native country.

With proper training and placement, however, nannies can find their jobs to be pleasant, satisfying experiences.

THE JOB

Nannies perform their child care duties in the homes of the families that employ them. Unlike other kinds of household help, nannies are specifically concerned with the needs of the children in their charge. Nannies prepare nutritious, appealing, and appetizing meals for the children. They may do grocery shopping specifically for the children.

Nannies may attend the children during their mealtimes and oversee their training in table manners and proper etiquette. They also clean up after the children's meals. If there is an infant in the family, a nanny will wash and sterilize bottles and feed the infant. It is not part of a nanny's regular duties to cook for the adult members of the household or do domestic chores outside of those required for the children.

Nannies are responsible for keeping order in the children's quarters. They may clean the bedrooms, nursery, and playrooms, making sure beds are made with clean linens and sufficient blankets. Nannies may also wash and iron the children's clothing and do any necessary mending. They make sure that the clothing is neatly put away. With older children, the nanny may begin instructions in orderliness and neatness, teaching children how to organize their possessions.

Nannies bathe and dress the children and instill proper grooming skills. Children often seek the assistance of their nanny in getting ready for family parties or holidays. As the children get older, nannies help them learn how to dress themselves and take care of their appearance.

Not only are nannies responsible for the care and training of their charges, but they also act as companions and guardians. They plan games and learning activities for the children and supervise their play, encouraging fairness and good sportsmanship. They may be responsible for planning activities to commemorate holidays, special events, or birthdays. These activities may center on field trips, arts and crafts, or parties. Nannies may travel with families on trips and vacations, or they may take the children on short excursions without their families. Nannies must be detail oriented when it comes to the children entrusted to their care. They keep records of illnesses, allergies, and injuries. They also note learning skills and related progress as well as personal achievements, such as abilities in games or arts and crafts. Later, they relate these events and achievements to the parents.

Nannies act as the parents' assistants by focusing closely on the children and fostering the behavior expected of them. They are responsible for carrying out the parents' directions for care and activities. By setting good examples and helping the children follow guidelines established by their parents, nannies encourage the development of happy and confident personalities.

REQUIREMENTS
High School
Nannies usually are required to have at least a high school diploma or equivalent (GED). Helpful high school classes include health,

psychology, and home economics. English and communications classes also are useful, as they provide skills that will help in everyday dealings with the children and their parents. Nannies usually must also have a valid driver's license, since they may be asked to chauffeur the children to doctors' appointments or other outings.

Postsecondary Training
There are several schools that offer specialized nanny training usually lasting between 12 and 16 weeks. These programs are typically accredited by individual state agencies. Employers generally prefer applicants who have completed an accredited program. Graduates of accredited programs also can command higher salaries.

Two- and four-year programs are available at many colleges and include courses on early childhood education, child growth and development, and child care. College course work in nanny training may also focus on communication, family health, first aid, child psychology, and food and nutrition. Classes may include play and recreational games, arts and crafts, children's literature, and safety and health. Because nannies may be responsible for children of various ages, the course work focuses on each stage of childhood development and the particular needs of individual children. Special emphasis is given to the care of infants. Professional nanny schools may also give instruction on family management, personal appearance, and appropriate conduct.

Certification or Licensing
The International Nanny Association (INA) offers a multiple-choice credentialing exam that allows nannies to demonstrate their expertise in the following areas: child development, family/provider communication, child guidance, multicultural/diversity awareness, learning environment, personal qualities of a nanny, safety, management skills health, nutrition, and professionalism. Earning the INA credential shows potential employers your commitment to the work as well as your level of training.

Other Requirements
Nannies must possess an even and generous temperament when working with children. They must be kind, affectionate, and genuinely interested in the child's well-being and development. Good physical condition, energy, and stamina are also necessary for success in this career. Nannies must be able to work well on their own initiative and have sound judgment to handle any small crises or emergencies that arise. They must know how to instill discipline and carry out the parents' expectations.

They should be loyal and committed to the children and respect the families for whom they work. In some cases, this is difficult, since nannies are often privy to negative elements of family life, including the emotional problems of parents and their neglect of their children. Nannies need to recognize that they are not part of the family and should not allow themselves to become too familiar with its members. When they disagree with the family on matters of raising the children, they should do so with tact and the realization that they are only employees. Finally, it is imperative that they be discreet about confidential family matters. A nanny who gossips about family affairs is likely to be rapidly dismissed.

EXPLORING

Baby-sitting is an excellent way to gain child care experience. Often, a baby-sitter cares for children without any supervision, thereby learning child management and personal responsibility. Volunteer or part-time work at day care centers, nurseries, or elementary schools can also be beneficial.

Talk to a nanny to get further information. There are several placement agencies for prospective nannies, and one of them might be able to set up a meeting or phone interview with someone who works in the field.

Gather information about nannies either from the library or from sources listed at the end of this article.

EMPLOYERS

Mid- to upper-income parents who seek in-home child care for their children usually employ nannies. These opportunities are generally available across the country in large cities and affluent suburbs. Most nannies are placed in homes by placement agencies, by employment agencies, or through government-authorized programs.

STARTING OUT

Most schools that train nannies offer placement services. In addition, it is possible to register with an employment agency that places child care workers. Currently, there are more than 200 agencies that specialize in placing nannies. Some agencies conduct recruitment drives or fairs to find applicants. Newspaper classified ads may also list job openings for nannies.

Prospective nannies should screen potential employers carefully. Applicants should ask for references from previous nannies, particularly if a family has had many prior nannies, and talk with one or more of them, if possible. There are many horror stories in nanny circles about past employers, and the prospective worker should not assume that every employer is exactly as he or she appears to be at first. Nannies also need to make sure that the specific duties and terms of the job are explicitly specified in a contract. Most agencies will supply sample contracts.

ADVANCEMENT

More than half of the nannies working in this country are under the age of 30. Many nannies work in child care temporarily as a way to support themselves through school. Many nannies leave their employers to start families of their own. Some nannies, as their charges grow older and start school, may be employed by a new family every few years. This may result in better-paying positions.

Other advancement opportunities for nannies depend on the personal initiative of the nanny. Some nannies enroll in college to get the necessary training to become teachers or child psychologists. Other nannies may establish their own child care agencies or schools for nannies.

EARNINGS

According to the U.S. Department of Labor, child care workers providing residential care (a group that includes nannies) had median hourly earnings of $9.97 in 2004. A person making this wage and working full-time at 40 hours a week would have a yearly income of approximately $20,750. The department also reports that of all child care workers in 2004, 10 percent earned less than $5.93 per hour (approximately $12,330 per year), and 10 percent earn more than $12.55 per hour (approximately $26,100 per year).

In reality, however, nannies often work more than 40 hours per week, and their pay may not be based on an hourly rate, but rather be a flat amount that may range from $250 to $400 or more per week. These weekly earnings translate into yearly incomes ranging from $13,000 to $20,800 or more. Income also depends on such factors as the number of children, length of time with a family, and level of previous experience. Some employers provide room and board but in return offer lower pay. Presently, the highest demands for nannies are in large cities on the west and east coasts. High demand can result in higher wages.

Some nannies may be asked to travel with the family. If it is a business-oriented trip, a nanny may be compensated with wages as well as additional days off upon return. If the travel is for vacation, a nanny may get paid a bonus for working additional days. Some employers choose not to take their nannies along when they travel, and these nannies may not earn any wages while the family is gone. Such situations can be a financial disadvantage for the nanny who has been promised full-time work and full-time pay. It is recommended that nannies anticipate possible scenarios or situations that may affect their working schedules and wages and discuss these issues with employers in advance.

Nannies often have work contracts with their families that designate wages, requirements, fringe benefits, and salary increases. Health insurance, worker's compensation, and Social Security tax are sometimes included in the benefits package. Annual pay raises vary, with increases of 7 or 8 percent being on the high end of the scale.

WORK ENVIRONMENT

No other job involves as intimate a relationship with other people and their children as the nanny's job. Because nannies often live with their employers, it is important that they choose their employer with as much care as the employer chooses them. All necessary working conditions need to be negotiated at the time of hire. Nannies should be fair, flexible, and able to adapt to changes easily. Because nannies work in their employers' homes, their working conditions vary greatly. Some nannies are live-ins, sharing the home of their employer because of convenience or because of the number or age of children in the family. Newborn babies require additional care that may require the nanny to live on the premises.

It is also common for nannies to live with their families during the week and return to their homes on the weekends. When nannies live in the family's home, they usually have their own quarters or a small apartment that is separate from the rest of the family's bedrooms and offers some privacy. Sometimes the nanny's room is next to the children's room so it is possible for the nanny to respond immediately if help is needed.

Nannies who are not live-ins may expect to stay at the home for long periods of time, much longer than a traditional nine-to-five job. Since it often is the nanny's responsibility to put the children to bed in the evening, a nanny may not return home until late evening. Often nannies are asked to stay late or work weekends if the parents have other engagements.

The work of a nanny can often be stressful or unpleasant. Many employers expect their nannies to do things unrelated to their job, such as clean the house, run errands, walk dogs, or baby-sit for neighborhood children. Some employers may be condescending, rude, and critical. Some mothers, while they need and want the services of a nanny, grow resentful and jealous of the bonds the nanny forms with the children.

Nannies have very few legal rights with regard to their jobs and have little recourse to deal with unfair employers. Job security is very poor, as parents have less need for nannies as their children get older and start school. In addition, nannies are often fired with no notice and sometimes no explanation due to the whims of their employers. Leaving behind a job and the children they have taken care of and grown close to can be emotionally difficult for workers in this field.

The work is often strenuous, requiring a great deal of lifting, standing, and walking or running. The work is also mentally taxing, as young children demand constant attention and energy. However, it can be very rewarding for nannies as they grow close to the children, helping with their upbringing and care. In the best cases, the nanny becomes an integral part of the family he or she works for and is treated with professionalism, respect, and appreciation.

OUTLOOK

The U.S. Department of Labor predicts that employment for all child care workers will grow about as fast as the average through 2012. The department notes, however, that job opportunities for nannies should be particularly good. The continuing trend of both parents working outside the home ensures that nannies will remain in demand. Even if many of these parents switch to part-time jobs, there will still be a need for qualified child care providers. Presently, the demand for nannies outweighs the supply, and graduating nannies may find themselves faced with several job offers. In addition, the long hours and low pay make for a high turnover rate in this field, and replacement workers are in steady demand. It may be years before the gap between the number of positions open and the availability of nannies diminishes.

FOR MORE INFORMATION

The following is an institution for the education and placement of certified professional nannies and certified professional governesses. For more information, contact
English Nanny and Governess School
37 South Franklin Street
Chagrin Falls, OH 44022
Tel: 800-733-1984
Email: admissions@nanny-governess.com
http://www.nanny-governess.com

The following organization is an exchange program that places foreign students between the ages of 18 and 26 in American homes as au pairs for one year. For more information, contact
GoAuPair
151 East 6100 South Suite 200
Murray, UT 84107
Tel: 888-287-2471
Email: inforequest@goaupair.com
http://www.goaupair.com

For information on a career as a nanny, earnings, and its credentialing exam, contact
International Nanny Association
2020 Southwest Freeway, Suite 208
Houston, TX 77098
Tel: 888-878-1477
http://www.nanny.org

The following organization is a national support group run by nannies for nannies. For information on their national network, newsletters, and yearly conferences, contact
National Association of Nannies
PMB 2004
25 Route 31 South, Suite C
Pennington, NJ 08534
Tel: 800-344-6266
Email: info@nannyassociation.com
http://www.nannyassociation.com

Neonatal Nurses

QUICK FACTS

School Subjects
Biology
Chemistry

Personal Interests
Helping/teaching
Technical/scientific

Work Environment
Primarily indoors
Primarily one location

Minimum Education Level
Some postsecondary training

Salary Range
$38,050 to $56,630 to
$77,170

Certification or Licensing
Required by all states

Outlook
Faster than the average

DOT
075

GOE
14.02.01

NOC
3152

O*NET-SOC
29-1111.00

OVERVIEW

Neonatal nurses provide direct patient care to newborns in hospitals for the first month after birth. The babies they care for may be normal, they may be born prematurely, or they may be suffering from an illness or birth defect. Some of the babies require highly technical care such as surgery or the use of ventilators, incubators, or intravenous feedings.

HISTORY

Neonatal care in some basic form has been around since the dawn of time. But the specialized field of neonatal nursing did not develop until the 1960s as advancements in medical care and technology allowed for the improved treatment of premature babies. According to the March of Dimes, one of every 13 babies born in the United States annually suffers from low birth weight. Low birth weight is a factor in 65 percent of infant deaths. Neonatal nurses play a very important role in providing care for these infants, those born with birth defects or illness, and healthy babies.

THE JOB

Neonatal nurses care for newborn babies in hospitals. Depending on the size of the hospital, their duties may vary. Some neonatal nurses may be in the delivery room and, as soon as the baby is born, they are responsible for cleaning up the baby, visually assessing it, and drawing blood by pricking the newborn's heel. This blood sample is sent to the laboratory, where a number of screening tests are performed as required by the state. These assessments help the staff and doctor determine if the baby is normal or needs additional testing, a special diet, or intensive

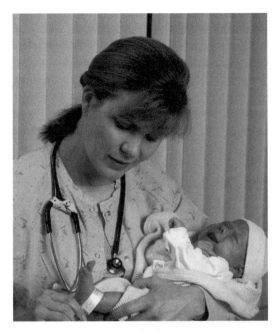

A neonatal nurse cares for a newborn baby. (Jim Whitmer Photography)

care. Sharon Stout, R.N., who was a neonatal nurse for six years in Georgia, said she loved being in the delivery room and caring for the newborn because she enjoyed seeing the interaction with the baby and the new mother and family. "It was usually a very happy time."

"However," she says, "if a baby needed special care that we could not provide at our facility, we stabilized it until the neonatal transport team arrived from a larger hospital to transfer the baby to its special neonatal care unit."

Babies who are born without complications are usually placed in a Level I nursery or in the mother's room with her. However, because of today's short hospital stays for mother and child, many hospitals no longer have Level I, or healthy baby nurseries. Neonatal or general staff nurses help the new mothers care for their newborns in their hospital rooms.

Level II is a special care nursery for babies who have been born prematurely or who may have an illness, disease, or birth defect. These babies are also cared for by a neonatal nurse, or a staff nurse with more advanced training in caring for newborns. These babies may need oxygen, intravenous therapies, special feedings, or, because of underdevelopment, they may simply need more time to mature.

Specialized neonatal nurses or more advanced degree nurses care for babies placed in the Level III neonatal intensive care unit. This unit admits all babies who cannot be treated in either of the other two nurseries. These at-risk babies require high-tech care such as ventilators, incubators, or surgery. Level III units are generally found in larger hospitals or may be part of a children's hospital.

REQUIREMENTS

High School

In order to become a neonatal nurse, you must first train to be a registered nurse. To prepare for a career as a registered nurse, you should take high school mathematics and science courses, including biology, chemistry, and physics. Health courses will also be helpful. English and speech courses should not be neglected because you must be able to communicate well with patients.

Postsecondary Training

There are three basic kinds of training programs that you may choose from to become a registered nurse: associate's degree, diploma, and bachelor's degree. Which of the three training programs to choose depends on your career goals. A bachelor's degree in nursing is required for most supervisory or administrative positions, for jobs in public health agencies, and for admission to graduate nursing programs. A master's degree is usually necessary to prepare for a nursing specialty or to teach. For some specialties, such as nursing research, a Ph.D. is essential.

There are approximately 678 bachelor's degree programs in nursing in the United States. It requires four (in some cases, five) years to complete. The graduate of this program receives a bachelor of science in nursing (B.S.N.) degree. The associate degree in nursing (A.D.N.) is awarded after completion of a two-year study program that is usually offered in a junior or community college. There are approximately 700 A.D.N. programs in the United States. You receive hospital training at cooperating hospitals in the general vicinity of the community college. The diploma program, which usually lasts three years, is conducted by hospitals and independent schools, although the number of these programs is declining. At the conclusion of each of these programs, you become a graduate nurse, but not, however, a registered nurse. All states require nurses to pass a licensing exam in order to receive the designation registered nurse.

There is no special program for neonatal nursing in basic registered nurse education; however, some nursing programs have an elective course in neonatal nursing. Entry-level requirements to become a neonatal nurse depend on the institution, its size, and the availability of nurses in that specialty and geographic region. Some institutions may require neonatal nurses to demonstrate their ability in administering medications, performing necessary math calculations, suctioning, cardiopulmonary resuscitation, ventilator care, and other newborn care skills. Nurses who wish to focus on caring for premature babies or sick newborns may choose to attend graduate school to become a neonatal nurse practitioner or clinical nurse specialist.

Certification or Licensing

Neonatal nurses who work in critical care may become certified in neonatal critical care nursing by the AACN Certification Corporation, a subsidiary of the American Association of Critical Care Nurses (AACN). Applicants must have a minimum of 1,750 hours within the two years preceding application (with 875 hours in the year previous to application), pay an application fee, and take and pass a four-hour exam.

Other Requirements

Neonatal nurses should like working with mothers, newborns, and families. This is a very intense nursing field, especially when caring for the high-risk infant, so the neonatal nurse should be compassionate, patient, and able to handle stress and make decisions. The nurse should also be able to communicate well with other medical staff and the patients' families. Families of an at-risk newborn are often frightened and very worried about their infant. Because of their fears, family members may be difficult to deal with, and the nurse must display patience, understanding, and composure during these emotional times. The nurse must be able to communicate with the family and explain medical terminology and procedures to them so they understand what is being done for their baby and why.

EXPLORING

You can explore your interest in neonatal nursing by reading books on careers in nursing; by talking with high school guidance counselors and neonatal nurses; and by visiting hospitals to observe a health care setting and talk with hospital personnel.

EMPLOYERS

Neonatal nurses are employed by hospitals, managed-care facilities, long-term-care facilities, and government agencies.

STARTING OUT

The only way to become a registered nurse is through completion of one of the three kinds of educational programs plus passing the licensing examination. Registered nurses may apply for employment directly to hospitals, nursing homes, and companies and government agencies that hire nurses. Jobs can also be obtained through school placement offices, by signing up with employment agencies specializing in placement of nursing personnel, or through the state employment office. Other sources of jobs include nurses' associations, professional journals, and newspaper want ads.

ADVANCEMENT

Neonatal nurses seeking career advancement, but who would like to continue to care for babies, might consider becoming a neonatal nurse practitioner or clinical nurse specialist. They can do this by gaining at least two years of experience in a neonatal intensive care unit (recommended by the National Association of Neonatal Nurses) and then completing graduate school training in their desired specialty.

EARNINGS

Salary is determined by many factors, including nursing specialty, education, place of employment, shift worked, geographic location, and work experience. According to the U.S. Department of Labor, registered nurses working at hospitals had a mean annual income of $56,630 in 2004. The lowest paid 10 percent of all registered nurses earned less than $38,050 per year. The highest paid 10 percent made more than $77,170. However, neonatal specialty nurses can generally expect to earn more, especially when advancing to administrative positions. According to the National Association of Neonatal Nurses, nurses just starting out in this field may have starting salaries in the upper $30,000s to mid-$40,000s. Given these high beginning salaries, it is logical to expect a neonatal nurse with some experience to earn more than the national median for all registered nurses.

Flexible schedules and part-time employment opportunities are available for most nurses. Employers usually provide health and life insurance, and some offer educational reimbursements and year-end bonuses to their full-time staff.

WORK ENVIRONMENT

Neonatal nurses can expect to work in a hospital environment that is clean and well lighted. Inner-city hospitals may be in a less than desirable location, and safety may be an issue. Generally, neonatal nurses who wish to advance in their careers will find themselves working in larger hospitals in major cities.

Nurses usually spend much of the day on their feet, either walking or standing. Many hospital nurses work 10- or 12-hour shifts, which can be tiring. Long hours and intense nursing demands can create burnout for some nurses, meaning that they often become dissatisfied with their jobs. Fortunately, there are many areas in which nurses can use their skills, so sometimes trying a different type of nursing may be the answer.

OUTLOOK

The U.S. Department of Labor predicts that employment for all registered nurses will grow faster than the average through 2012. In addition, nursing specialties should be in great demand in the future. The outlook for neonatal nurses is very good, especially for those with master's degrees or higher. According to the National Association of Neonatal Nurses, positions should be available due to downsizing in previous years. These cutbacks have led to a decrease in the number of nurses choosing advanced practice education. Also, the average neonatal nurse today is middle-aged and may be moving on to less stressful areas of nursing.

FOR MORE INFORMATION

For information on training, contact
American Association of Colleges of Nursing
One Dupont Circle, NW, Suite 530
Washington, DC 20036
Tel: 202-463-6930
Email: info@aacn.nche.edu
http://www.aacn.nche.edu

For information on certification, contact
AACN Certification Corporation
American Association of Critical-Care Nurses
101 Columbia
Aliso Viejo, CA 92656-4109
Tel: 800-899-2226
Email: info@aacn.org
http://www.aacn.org

For information on neonatal nursing, contact
Association of Women's Health, Obstetric and Neonatal Nurses
2000 L Street, NW, Suite 740
Washington, DC 20036
Tel: 800-673-8499
http://www.awhonn.org

For career information and job listings, contact
National Association of Neonatal Nurses
4700 West Lake Avenue
Glenview, IL 60025-1485
Tel: 800-451-3795
Email: info@nann.org
http://www.nann.org

Pediatricians

OVERVIEW

Pediatricians are physicians who provide health care to infants, children, and adolescents. Typically, a pediatrician meets a new patient soon after birth and takes care of that patient through his or her teenage years. There are nearly 27,000 pediatricians employed in the United States.

HISTORY

Children became the focus of separate medical care during the 18th century in Europe. Children's health care became a recognized medical specialty during the early 19th century, and by the middle of the 19th century, pediatrics was taught separately in medical schools. The first pediatric clinic in the United States opened in New York City in 1862. About that same time, several children's hospitals opened in Europe.

Studies focused on developing treatments for infectious diseases of childhood such as measles and scarlet fever. By the beginning of the 20th century, pediatricians began promoting the normal growth and development of children. Well-child clinics began to open around the United States.

Some of the most significant breakthroughs in children's health care have been in disease prevention. By the middle of the 20th century, the development of vaccines and antibiotics greatly decreased the threat of infectious diseases.

QUICK FACTS

School Subjects
Biology
Health

Personal Skills
Helping/teaching
Technical/scientific

Work Environment
Primarily indoors
Primarily multiple locations

Minimum Education Level
Medical degree

Salary Range
$95,000 to $135,450 to
$201,086

Certification or Licensing
Recommended (certification)
Required by all states
(licensing)

Outlook
About as fast as the average

DOT
070

GOE
14.02.01

NOC
3112

O*NET-SOC
29-1065.00

THE JOB

A significant part of a pediatrician's job is preventive medicine—what is sometimes called "well care." This involves periodically seeing a patient for routine health checkups. During these checkups, the doctor physically examines the child to make sure he or she is growing at a normal rate and to look for symptoms of illness. The physical examination includes testing reflexes, listening to the heart and lungs, checking eyes and ears, and measuring height and weight.

During the checkup, the pediatrician also assesses the child's mental and behavioral development. This is done both by observing the patient's behavior and by asking the parents questions about their child's abilities.

Immunizing children against certain childhood diseases is another important part of preventive medicine. Pediatricians administer routine immunizations for such diseases as rubella, polio, and smallpox as children reach certain ages. Yet another part of preventive medicine is family education. Pediatricians counsel and advise parents on the care and treatment of their children. They provide information on such parental concerns as safety, diet, and hygiene.

In addition to practicing preventive medicine, pediatricians also treat sick infants and children. When a sick or injured patient is brought into the office, the doctor examines him or her, makes a diagnosis, and orders treatment. Common ailments include ear infections, allergies, feeding difficulties, viral illnesses, respiratory illnesses, and gastrointestinal upsets. For these and other illnesses, pediatricians prescribe and administer treatments and medications.

If a patient is seriously ill or hurt, a pediatrician arranges for hospital admission and follows up on the patient's progress during the hospitalization. In some cases, a child may have a serious condition, such as cancer, cystic fibrosis, or hemophilia, that requires the attention of a specialist. In these cases, the pediatrician, as the primary care physician, will refer the child to the appropriate specialist.

Some pediatric patients may be suffering from emotional or behavioral disorders or from substance abuse. Other patients may be affected by problems within their families, such as unemployment, alcoholism, or physical abuse. In these cases, pediatricians may make referrals to such health professionals as psychiatrists, psychologists, and social workers.

Some pediatricians choose to pursue pediatric subspecialties, such as the treatment of children who have heart disorders, kidney disorders, or cancer. Subspecialization requires a longer residency training than does general practice. A pediatrician practicing a subspecialty typically spends a much greater proportion of his or her time in a hospital or medical center than does a general practice pediatrician. Subspecialization permits pediatricians to be involved in research activities.

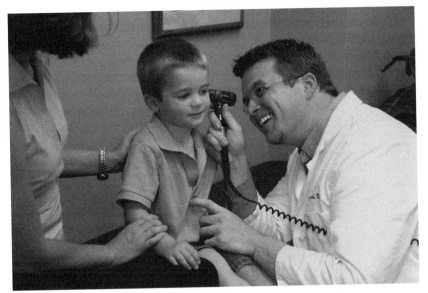

A pediatrician examines the ear of a young boy who had been complaining of ringing in his ears. *(Jim Whitmer Photography)*

REQUIREMENTS

High School
While in high school, take college prep classes, with a heavy emphasis on science and math. Biology, chemistry, physics, and physiology are important science classes. Any advanced math courses are also excellent choices.

Classes in English, foreign languages, and speech will enhance communication skills, which are vital to being a successful physician. Social sciences such as psychology and sociology, which increase your understanding of others, are also beneficial.

Postsecondary Training
To begin a career as a physician you need to first enter a liberal arts or science program in an accredited undergraduate institution. Some colleges offer a premedical course, but a good general education, with as many science courses as possible and a major in biology or chemistry, is considered adequate preparation for the study of medicine. Courses should include physics, biology, inorganic and organic chemistry, English, mathematics, and the social sciences.

College students should begin to apply to medical schools early in their senior year, so it is advisable to begin your research into schools as early as your freshman year. There are 126 accredited schools of medicine and 20 accredited schools of osteopathic medicine in the country. For more information, consult a copy of *Medical School Admission Requirements, United States and Canada,* available from the Association of American Medical Colleges or from your college library. This publication is updated each spring.

Some students may be admitted to medical school after only three years of study in an undergraduate program. There are a few medical schools that award the bachelor's degree at the end of the first year of medical school study. This practice is becoming less common as more students seek admission to medical schools. Most premedical students plan to spend four years in an undergraduate program and to receive the bachelor's degree before entering the four-year medical school program.

During your second or third year in college, you should arrange with an adviser to take the Medical College Admission Test (MCAT). This test is given each spring and each fall. Your adviser should know the date, place, and time; or you may write for this information to the Association of American Medical Colleges. All medical colleges in the United States require this test for admission, and a student's MCAT score is one of the factors that is weighed in the decision to accept or reject any applicant. The examination covers four areas: verbal facility, quantitative ability, knowledge of the humanities and social sciences, and knowledge of biology, chemistry, and physics.

You are encouraged to apply to at least three institutions to increase your chances of being accepted by one of them. Approximately one out of every two qualified applicants to medical schools is admitted each year. To facilitate this process, the American Medical College Application Service (AMCAS) will check, copy, and submit applications to the medical schools you specify. More information about this service may be obtained from AMCAS, premedical advisers, and medical schools.

In addition to the traditional medical schools, there are several schools of basic medical sciences that enroll medical students for the first two years (preclinical experience) of medical school. They offer a preclinical curriculum to students similar to that which is offered by regular medical schools. At the end of the two-year program, you can apply to a four-year medical school for the final two years of instruction.

Although high scholarship is a deciding factor in admitting a student to a medical school, it is actually only one of the criteria considered. By far the greatest number of successful applicants to medical schools are "B" students. Because admission is also determined by a number of other factors, including a personal interview, other qualities in addition to a high scholastic average are considered desirable for a prospective physician. High on the list of desirable qualities are emotional stability, integrity, reliability, resourcefulness, and a sense of service.

The average student enters medical school at age 21 or 22. Then you begin another four years of formal schooling. During the first two years of medical school, studies include human anatomy, biochemistry, physiology, pharmacology, psychology, microbiology, pathology, medical ethics, and laws governing medicine. Most instruction in the first two years is given through classroom lectures, laboratories, seminars, independent research, and the reading of textbook material and other types of literature. You also learn to take medical histories, examine patients, and recognize symptoms.

During the last two years in medical school, you become actively involved in the treatment process. You spend a large proportion of the time in the hospital as part of a medical team headed by a teaching physician who specializes in a particular area. Others on the team may be interns or residents. You are closely supervised as you learn techniques such as how to take a patient's medical history, how to conduct a physical examination, how to work in the laboratory, how to make a diagnosis, and how to keep all the necessary records.

As you rotate from one medical specialty to another, you obtain a broad understanding of each field. You are assigned to duty in internal medicine, pediatrics, psychiatry, obstetrics and gynecology, surgery, and other specialties.

In addition to this hospital work, you continue to take courses. You are responsible for assigned studies and also for some independent study.

After earning an M.D. degree and becoming licensed to practice medicine, pediatricians must complete a three-year residency program in a hospital. The pediatric residency provides extensive experience in ambulatory pediatrics, the care of infants and children who are not bedridden. Residents also spend time working in various specialized pediatric units, including neonatology, adolescent medicine, child development, psychology, special care, intensive care, and outpatient.

Some of the other subspecialties a pediatrician might acquire training for include adolescent medicine, *pediatric cardiology* (care of children with heart disease), *pediatric critical care* (care of children requiring advanced life support), *pediatric endocrinology* (care of children with diabetes and other glandular disorders), *pediatric neurology* (care of children with nervous system disorders), and *pediatric hematology/oncology* (care of children with blood disorders and cancer).

Certification or Licensing

Certification by the American Board of Pediatrics is recommended. A certificate in General Pediatrics is awarded after three years of residency training and the successful completion of a two-day comprehensive written examination. A pediatrician who specializes in cardiology, infectious diseases, or other areas must complete an additional three-year residency in the subspecialty before taking the certification examination.

Other Requirements

To be a successful pediatrician, you should like children and adolescents; have patience, compassion, and a good sense of humor; be willing to continually learn; have a desire to help others; and be able to withstand stress and make sound decisions.

EXPLORING

There are many ways you can prepare for medical school and a career in pediatrics. Participation in science clubs, for example, will allow for in-depth explorations of some areas of science. Volunteer work at hospitals or other health care institutions will allow you to see many aspects of medical care. Such volunteer work can also provide a taste of what a physician's career entails, and help you decide if you is suited for it. You can also ask your science teacher or counselor to arrange an information interview with a pediatrician to see if this career is a good fit for you.

EMPLOYERS

The majority of the nearly 27,000 pediatricians in the United States are involved in direct patient care. Of these, about one-third have private practices. The others work in group practices, community clinics, hospitals, university-affiliated medical centers, and health maintenance organizations. Only about 10 percent of pediatricians work in administration, teaching, or research.

STARTING OUT

There are no shortcuts to entering the medical profession. Requirements are an M.D. degree, a licensing examination, a one- or two-year internship, and a three-year residency. Upon completing this program, which may take up to 15 years, pediatricians are then ready to enter practice.

For the pediatrician who plans to set up a private practice, it is wise to consult with his or her medical school career services office to find a suitable geographic location in which to do so. Certain locations, such as rural areas and small towns, offer less competition for patients and, therefore, better chances of success.

Many newly licensed pediatricians take salaried jobs until they can pay off some of their medical school debt, which is likely to total more than $50,000. Medical school career services offices should be able to recommend hospitals, clinics, HMOs, and group practices that are hiring pediatricians.

ADVANCEMENT

The most common method of advancement for pediatricians is subspecialization. There are several subspecialties open to the pediatrician who is willing to spend the additional time training for one. A subspecialty requires three more years of residency training.

Some subspecialties a pediatrician might train for include *neonatology* (the care of sick newborns), adolescent medicine, pediatric cardiology, pediatric critical care, pediatric endocrinology, pediatric neurology (care of children with nervous system disorders), and pediatric hematology/oncology.

Some pediatricians pursue careers in research. Possible research activities include developing new vaccines for infections, developing treatments for children with heart disease, and developing treatments for infants born with severe abnormalities.

Another way for pediatricians to advance is to move into the field of education, where they can teach medical students and resident physicians about particular areas of pediatrics.

EARNINGS

Pediatricians, while at the low end of the earning scale for physicians, still have among the highest earnings of any occupation in the United States.

According to the U.S. Department of Labor, pediatricians had median earnings of $135,450 in 2004. According to PhysiciansSearch.com, pediatricians receive starting salaries that range from $95,000 to $145,000. Those with three years of experience earn salaries that are as high as $201,086. The earnings of pediatricians are partly dependent upon the types of practices they choose. Those who are self-employed tend to earn more than those who are salaried. Geographic region, hours worked, number of years in practice, professional reputation, and personality are other factors that can affect a pediatrician's income.

WORK ENVIRONMENT

Pediatricians that are in general practice usually work alone or in partnership with other physicians. Their average workweek is 50 to 60 hours, most of which is spent seeing patients in their offices. They also make hospital rounds to visit any of their patients who have been admitted for treatment or to check on newborn patients and their mothers. Pediatricians spend some time on call, taking care of patients who have emergencies. A pediatrician might be called to attend the delivery of a baby, to meet an injured patient in the emergency room, or simply to answer a parent's question about a sick child.

Some pediatricians choose to pursue pediatric subspecialties, such as the treatment of children who have heart disorders, kidney disorders, or cancer. A pediatrician practicing a subspecialty typically spends a much greater proportion of his or her time in a hospital or medical center than does a general practice pediatrician. Subspecialization permits pediatricians to be involved in research activities.

OUTLOOK

According to the *Occupational Outlook Handbook*, jobs for physicians are expected to grow about as fast as the average through 2012. The employment prospects for pediatricians—along with other general practitioners, such as family physicians—are especially good. This is because of the increasing use of managed care plans that stress preventive care.

FOR MORE INFORMATION

For more information on ambulatory pediatric care, contact
Ambulatory Pediatric Association
6728 Old McLean Village Drive
McLean, VA 22101
Tel: 703-556-9222
Email: info@ambpeds.org
http://www.ambpeds.org

To read Pediatric 101: A useful career guide, *visit the Academy's website.*
American Academy of Pediatrics
141 Northwest Point Boulevard
Elk Grove Village, IL 60007-1098
Tel: 847-434-4000
http://www.aap.org/profed/career.htm

For information on board certification, contact
American Board of Pediatrics
111 Silver Cedar Court
Chapel Hill, NC 27514
Tel: 919-929-0461
Email: abpeds@abpeds.org
http://www.abp.org/abpfr.htm

To read publications on pediatric care, visit the society's website.
American Pediatric Society
3400 Research Forest Drive, Suite B-7
The Woodlands, TX 77381
Tel: 281-419-0052
Email: info@aps-spr.org
http://www.aps-spr.org

Preschool Teachers

QUICK FACTS

School Subjects
Art
English
Family and consumer science

Personal Skills
Communication/ideas
Helping/teaching

Work Environment
Primarily indoors
Primarily one location

Minimum Education Level
Some postsecondary training

Salary Range
$14,540 to $21,550 to
$67,730

Certification or Licensing
Required for certain positions

Outlook
About as fast as the average

DOT
092

GOE
12.02.03

NOC
4142

O*NET-SOC
25-2011.00, 25-2012.00

OVERVIEW

Preschool teachers promote the general education of children under the age of five. They help students develop physically, socially, and emotionally, work with them on language and communications skills, and help cultivate their cognitive abilities. They also work with families to support parents in raising their young children and reinforcing skills at home. They plan and lead activities developed in accordance with the specific ages and needs of the children. It is the goal of all preschool teachers to help students develop the skills, interests, and individual creativity that they will use for the rest of their lives. Many schools and districts consider *kindergarten teachers,* who teach students five years of age, to be preschool teachers. For the purposes of this article, kindergarten teachers will be included in this category. There are approximately 424,000 preschool teachers and 168,000 kindergarten teachers in the United States.

HISTORY

Friedrich Froebel, a German educator, founded the first kindergarten ("child's garden" in German) in 1837 in Blankenburg, Germany. He also taught adults how to be kindergarten teachers. One of his adult students, Mrs. Carl Schurz, moved to the United States and started the first kindergarten in this country in Watertown, Wisconsin, in the mid-1800s. By 1873, St. Louis added the first American public kindergarten, and preschools for students under age five began to spring up in Europe around this same time. Preschools were introduced into the United States in the 1920s.

Preschool programs expanded rapidly in the United States during the 1960s, due in large part to the government instituting the Head Start program, designed to help preschool-aged children from low-income families receive educational and socialization opportunities and therefore be better prepared for elementary school. This program also allowed the parents of the children to work during the day. Around the same time, many U.S. public school systems began developing mandatory kindergarten programs for five-year-olds, and today many schools, both preschool and elementary, public and private, are offering full-day kindergarten programs.

THE JOB

Preschool teachers plan and lead activities that build on children's abilities and curiosity and aid them in developing skills and characteristics that help them grow. Because children develop at varying skill levels as well as have different temperaments, preschool teachers need to develop a flexible schedule with time allowed for music, art, playtime, academics, rest, and other activities.

Preschool teachers plan activities that encourage children to develop skills appropriate to their developmental needs. For example, they plan activities based on the understanding that a three-year-old child has different motor skills and reasoning abilities than a child of five years of age. They work with the youngest students on learning the days of the week and the recognition of colors, seasons, and animal names and characteristics. They help older students with number and letter recognition and even simple writing skills. Preschool teachers help children with such simple, yet important, tasks as tying shoelaces and washing hands before snack time. Attention to the individual needs of each child is vital; preschool teachers need to be aware of these needs and capabilities, and when possible, adapt activities to the specific needs of the individual child. Self-confidence and the development of communication skills are encouraged in preschools. For example, teachers may give children simple art projects, such as finger painting, and have children show and explain their finished projects to the rest of the class. Show and tell, or "sharing time" as it is often called, gives students opportunities to speak and listen to others.

"A lot of what I teach is based on social skills," says June Gannon, a preschool teacher in Amherst, New Hampshire. "During our circle time, we say hello to one another, sing songs, have show and tell, talk about the weather, and do calendar events. We then move on to language arts, which may include talking to children about rules, good listening, helping, sharing, etc., using puppets, work papers, games, and songs."

Preschool teachers adopt many parental responsibilities for the children. They greet the children in the morning and supervise them throughout the day. Often these responsibilities can be quite demanding and complicated. In harsh weather, for example, preschool teachers contend not only with boots, hats, coats, and mittens, but with the inevitable sniffles, colds, and generally cranky behavior that can occur in young children. For most children, preschool is their first time away from home and family for an extended period of time. A major portion of a preschool teacher's day is spent helping children adjust to being away from home and encouraging them to play together. This is especially true at the beginning of the school year. They may need to gently reassure children who become frightened or homesick.

In both full-day and half-day programs, preschool teachers supervise snack time, helping children learn how to eat properly and clean up after themselves. Proper hygiene, such as hand washing before meals, is also stressed. Other activities include storytelling, music, and simple arts and crafts projects. Full-day programs involve a lunch period and at least one nap time. Programs usually have exciting activities interspersed with calmer ones. Even though the children get nap time, preschool teachers must be energetic throughout the day, ready to face with good cheer the many challenges and demands of young children.

Preschool teachers also work with the parents of each child. It is not unusual for parents to come to preschool and observe a child or go on a field trip with the class, and preschool teachers often take these opportunities to discuss the progress of each child as well as any specific problems or concerns. Scheduled meetings are available for parents who cannot visit the school during the day. Solutions to fairly serious problems are worked out in tandem with the parents, often with the aid of the director of the preschool, or in the case of an elementary school kindergarten, with the principal or headmaster.

Kindergarten teachers usually have their own classrooms, made up exclusively of five-year-olds. Although these teachers don't have to plan activities for a wide range of ages, they need to consider individual developmental interests, abilities, and backgrounds represented by the students. Kindergarten teachers usually spend more time helping students with academic skills than do other preschool teachers. While a teacher of a two-, three-, and four-year-old classroom may focus more on socializing and building confidence in students through play and activities, kindergarten teachers often develop activities that help five-year-olds acquire the skills they will need in grade school, such as introductory activities on numbers, reading, and writing.

Preschool teachers must be patient and self-disciplined to manage large groups of students. (*Jim Whitmer Photography*)

REQUIREMENTS

High School
You should take child development, home economics, and other classes that involve you with child care, such as family and consumer science. You'll also need a fundamental understanding of the general subjects you'll be introducing to preschool students, so take English, science, and math. Also, take classes in art, music, and theater to develop creative skills.

Postsecondary Training
Specific education requirements for preschool and kindergarten teachers vary from state to state and also depend on the specific guidelines of the school or district. Many schools and child care centers require preschool teachers to have a bachelor's degree in early childhood education or a related field, but others accept adults with a high school diploma and some childcare experience. Some preschool facilities offer on-the-job training to their teachers, hiring them as assistants or aides until they are sufficiently trained to work in a classroom alone. A college degree program should include course work in a variety of liberal arts subjects, including English, history, and science as well as nutrition, child development, psychology of the young child, and sociology.

Several groups offer on-the-job training programs for prospective preschool teachers. For example, the American Montessori Society offers a career program for aspiring preschool teachers. This program requires a three-month classroom training period followed by one year of supervised on-the-job training.

Certification or Licensing

In some states, licensure may be required. Many states accept the child development associate credential (awarded by the Council for Professional Recognition) or an associate or bachelor's degree as sufficient requirements for work in a preschool facility. Individual state boards of education can provide specific licensure information. Kindergarten teachers working in public elementary schools almost always need teaching certification similar to that required by other elementary school teachers in the school. Other types of licensure or certification may be required, depending upon the school or district. These may include first-aid or cardiopulmonary resuscitation (CPR) training.

Other Requirements

Because young children look up to adults and learn through example, it is especially important that preschool teachers be good role models. "Remember how important your job is," June Gannon says. "Everything you say and do will affect these children." Gannon also emphasizes being respectful of the children and keeping a sense of humor. "I have patience and lots of heart for children," Gannon says. "You definitely need both."

EXPLORING

Preschools, daycare centers, and other childcare programs often hire high school students for part-time positions as aides. You may also find many volunteer opportunities to work with children. Check with your library or local literacy program about tutoring children and reading to preschoolers. Summer day camps or religious schools with preschool classes also hire high school students as counselors or counselors-in-training. Discussing the field with preschool teachers and observing in their classes are other good ways to discover specific job information and explore your aptitude for this career.

EMPLOYERS

There are approximately 424,000 preschool teachers employed in the United States, as well as 168,000 kindergarten teachers. Some 65 percent of women of children under the age of six are in the labor force, and the number is rising. Both government and the private sector are working to fill the enormous need for quality childcare. Preschool teachers will find many job opportunities in private and public preschools, including daycare centers, government-funded learning programs, churches, and Montessori schools. They may find work in a small center, or with a large preschool with many students and classrooms. Preschool franchises, like Primrose School Franchising Company and Kids 'R' Kids International, are also providing more opportunities for preschool teachers.

STARTING OUT

Before becoming a preschool teacher, June Gannon gained a lot of experience in child care. "I have worked as a special education aide and have taken numerous classes in childhood education," she says. "I am a sign language interpreter and have taught deaf children in a public school inclusion program."

If you hope to become a preschool teacher, you can contact child care centers, nursery schools, Head Start programs, and other preschool facilities to identify job opportunities. Often jobs for preschool teachers are listed in the classified section of newspapers. In addition, many school districts and state boards of education maintain job listings of available teaching positions. If no permanent positions are available at preschools, you may be able to find opportunities to work as a substitute teacher. Most preschools and kindergartens maintain a substitute list and refer to it frequently.

ADVANCEMENT

Many teachers advance by becoming more skillful in what they do. Skilled preschool teachers, especially those with additional training, usually receive salary increases as they become more experienced. A few preschool teachers with administrative ability and an interest in administrative work advance to the position of director. Administrators need to have at least a master's degree in child development or a related field and have to meet any state or federal licensing regulations. Some become directors of Head Start programs or other government programs. A relatively small number of experienced preschool teachers open their own facilities. This entails not only the ability to be an effective administrator but also the knowledge of how to operate a business. Kindergarten teachers sometimes have the opportunity to earn more money by teaching at a higher grade level in the elementary school. This salary increase is especially true when a teacher moves from a half-day kindergarten program to a full-day grade school classroom.

EARNINGS

Although there have been some attempts to correct the discrepancies in salaries between preschool teachers and other teachers, salaries in this profession tend to be lower than teaching positions in public elementary and high schools. Because some preschool programs are held only in the morning or afternoon, many preschool teachers work only part time. Thus, they often do not receive medical insurance or other benefits and may get paid minimum wage to start.

According to the U.S. Department of Labor, preschool teachers earned a median salary of $21,550 a year in 2004. Annual salaries for these workers ranged from less than $14,540 to $37,470 or more. The department reports that kindergarten teachers (which the department classifies separately from preschool teachers) earned median annual salaries of $42,050 in 2004. The lowest 10 percent earned less than $27,570, while the highest 10 percent earned $67,730 or more.

WORK ENVIRONMENT

Preschool teachers spend much of their workday on their feet in a classroom or on a playground. Facilities vary from a single room to large buildings. Class sizes also vary; some preschools serve only a handful of children, while others serve several hundred. Classrooms may be crowded and noisy, but anyone who loves children will enjoy all the activity. "The best part about working with children," Gannon says, "is the laughter, the fun, the enjoyment of watching the children grow physically, emotionally, and intellectually."

Many children do not go to preschool all day, so preschool teachers may work part time. Part-time employees generally work between 18 and 30 hours a week, while full-time employees work 35 to 40 hours a week. Part-time work gives the employee flexibility, and for many, this is one of the advantages of the job. Some preschool teachers teach both morning and afternoon classes, going through the same schedule and lesson plans with two sets of students.

OUTLOOK

Employment opportunities for preschool teachers are expected to increase about as fast as the average for all occupations through 2012, according to the U.S. Department of Labor. Specific job opportunities vary from state to state and depend on demographic characteristics and level of government funding. Jobs should be available at private child care centers, nursery schools, Head Start facilities, public and private kindergartens, and laboratory schools connected with universities and colleges. In the past, the majority of preschool teachers were female, and although this continues to be the case, more males are becoming involved in early childhood education.

One-third of all childcare workers leave their centers each year, often because of the low pay and lack of benefits. This will mean plenty of job openings for preschool teachers and possibly improved benefit plans, as centers attempt to maintain qualified preschool teachers.

Employment for all teachers, including preschool teachers, will vary by region and state. The U.S. Department of Labor predicts that Southern and Western states, particularly Georgia, California, Texas, Idaho, Hawaii, Alaska, and New Mexico, will have strong increases in enrollments, while schools located in the Northeast and Midwest may experience declines in enrollment.

FOR MORE INFORMATION

For information on training programs, contact
American Montessori Society
281 Park Avenue South
New York, NY 10010-6102
Tel: 212-358-1250
http://www.amshq.org

For information about certification, contact
Council for Professional Recognition
2460 16th Street, NW
Washington, DC 20009-3575
Tel: 800-424-4310
http://www.cdacouncil.org

For general information on preschool teaching careers, contact
National Association for the Education of Young Children
1509 16th Street, NW
Washington, DC 20036
Tel: 800-424-2460
http://www.naeyc.org

For information about student memberships and training opportunities, contact
National Association of Child Care Professionals
PO Box 90723
Austin, TX 78709-0723
Tel: 800-537-1118
Email: admin@naccp.org
http://www.naccp.org

School Nurses

QUICK FACTS

School Subjects
Biology
Chemistry

Personal Interests
Helping/teaching
Technical/scientific

Work Environment
Primarily indoors
One location with some travel

Minimum Education Level
Some postsecondary training

Salary Range
$24,910 to $53,640 to
$77,170+

Certification or Licensing
Required by some states
(certification)
Required (licensing)

Outlook
About as fast as the average

DOT
075

GOE
14.02.01

NOC
3152

O*NET/SOC
29-1111.00

OVERVIEW

School nurses focus on students' overall health. They may work in one school or in several, visiting each for a part of the day or week. They may also assist the school physician, if the school employs one. They work with parents, teachers, and other school and professional personnel to meet students' health needs. School nurses promote health and safety, work to prevent illnesses, treat accidents and minor injuries, maintain students' health records, and refer students who may need additional medical attention. School nurses may also be responsible for health education programs and school health plans. They are also in charge of administering medication to children and for seeing that special needs students' health requirements are met. School nurses are employed at the elementary, middle, and high school levels. There are about 57,000 registered nurses employed as school nurses in the United States.

HISTORY

According to the National Association of School Nurses, school nursing began in 1902 when registered nurse Lina Rogers was placed in the New York City school district as an "experiment." The Association reports that the experiment was a success, as the number of school children sent home as a result of illness declined the next year.

The National Association of School Nurses was formed (originally as the National Education Association's Department of School Nurses) in 1968 to represent the professional needs of school nurses. Its members seek to improve the health and performance of students in schools across the United States.

THE JOB

"Many people think school nursing is simply putting bandages on skinned knees, but it is much more than that," says Sue Schilb, R.N., a school nurse at an elementary school in Iowa for five years. "Of course, we take care of injured and sick children, but what most people don't realize is the amount of paperwork, planning, and record keeping that is involved in the job."

Schilb adds, "We must assess every child entering kindergarten and make sure the child has had all the required immunizations. In addition, we must maintain records on all the students, including state-mandated immunizations. We take the height and weight of each student every year, check their vision, and work with an audiologist to conduct hearing tests."

In addition to all the record keeping tasks, school nurses are frequently a resource for parents or staff members. "We often interact with parents when their children are ill or if they have questions about their child's health," says Schilb. "If special-needs children attend our school, we must develop a care plan for them to make sure their needs are met."

School nurses are also health educators. Teachers may ask the school nurse to speak to their individual classes when they are covering subjects that deal with health or safety. School nurses may also be required to make presentations on disease prevention, health education, and environmental health and safety to the student body, staff, and parent organizations.

School nurses may be employed on a full- or part-time basis depending on the school's needs, their funding, their size, and their state's or district's requirements. Some school nurses may also be employed in private or parochial schools.

REQUIREMENTS

High School

Take high school courses in mathematics and science courses, including biology, chemistry, and physics. Health courses will also be helpful. English and speech courses should not be neglected because you must be able to communicate well with patients.

Postsecondary Training

State requirements for school nurses vary. Some states have a certification requirement. Others require that their school nurses have bachelor's degrees while some do not require a bachelor's degree but do have specific educational requirements. There are some states that require their school nurses to be registered nurses.

Many school nurses are graduates of practical nursing programs, which involve about one year of classroom instruction and supervised clinical practice, which usually takes place in a hospital.

There are three basic kinds of training programs that you may choose from to become a registered nurse: associate degree, diploma, and bachelor's degree. Which of the three training programs to choose depends on your career goals. A bachelor's degree in nursing is the most popular method, however, as such a degree is required for most supervisory or administrative positions, for jobs in public health agencies, and for admission to graduate nursing programs. Diplomas are offered by three-year programs at schools of nursing and hospitals. Associate degrees can be obtained by attending a two-year college.

Certification or Licensing

Both licensed practical nurses and registered nurses must pass an examination after they have completed a state-approved nursing program. This is required by all states and the District of Columbia.

Currently 20 states have certification or licensing requirements for school nurses. National certification is available through the National Board for Certification of School Nurses. In addition, some state education agencies set requirements such as nursing experience and competency in specified areas of health and education. Local or regional boards of education may also have certain qualifications that they require of their school nurses.

Other Requirements

School nurses must have patience and like working with children and teens. They must also be able to work well with teachers, parents, administrators, and other health personnel. School nurses should be able to work independently since they often work alone.

EXPLORING

This is one area of nursing where you don't have far to travel to talk to someone in the career: visit your own school nurse. Ask about his or her daily responsibilities and workload and how he or she prepared for this line of work. Ask for suggestions on nursing programs and other tips on starting your career.

See if your school or local institution offers first-aid programs to learn some basic emergency medical procedures such as CPR.

Another way to gain experience is through volunteer work at a hospital, nursing home, or other medical facility.

EMPLOYERS

School nurses are employed by private and public schools at the elementary, middle, and high school levels.

STARTING OUT

Many new nurses gain practical experience in a non-school setting before they apply for employment as a school nurse. Nurses can apply directly to hospitals, nursing homes, and companies and government agencies that hire nurses. Jobs can also be obtained through school placement offices, by signing up with employment agencies specializing in placement of nursing personnel, or through state employment offices. Other sources of jobs include nurses' associations, professional journals, newspaper want ads, and Internet job sites.

ADVANCEMENT

Administrative and supervisory positions in the nursing field go to nurses who have earned at least the bachelor of science degree in nursing. Nurses with many years of experience who are graduates of a diploma program may achieve supervisory positions, but requirements for such promotions have become more difficult in recent years. In many cases supervisory positions require at least the bachelor of science in nursing degree.

Some school nurses may advance to the position of *registered school nurse*. These professionals manage and oversee health aides employed in the schools.

EARNINGS

According to the U.S. Department of Labor, registered nurses had median annual earnings of $53,640 in 2004. Salaries ranged from less than $38,050 to more than $77,170. Licensed practical nurses earned median salaries of $34,650 in 2004. The lowest paid 10 percent made less than $24,910, and the highest paid 10 percent made more than $47,440. School nurses' salaries may differ from these figures, however. School nurses' salaries are determined by several factors—the financial status of the school district, the nurse's experience, and their scope of duties.

WORK ENVIRONMENT

Schools are found in all communities, cities, and rural areas, and learning institutions can vary greatly. School nurses may work in an environment that is a state-of-the-art educational institution in an affluent community, or they may work in a rundown building in the inner city. By the same token, some school nurses may have up-to-date equipment and adequate resources, while others may find that they have restricted funds that inhibit their ability to do their jobs.

School nurses usually work days and may have some time off during the summer months when school is not in session.

The increase in school violence impacts the school nurses' working environment since it is evident that acts of violence can occur in any institution in any community. School nurses must be prepared to deal with the physical results of violence in their schools.

School nurses may come in contact with infectious diseases and are often exposed to illnesses and injuries. All nursing careers have some health and disease risks; however, adherence to health and safety guidelines greatly minimizes the chance of contracting infectious diseases such as hepatitis and AIDS.

OUTLOOK

Nursing specialties will be in great demand in the future. In fact, according to the U.S. Department of Labor, there will be more new jobs for registered nurses than for any other profession through 2012. From 2000 to 2012, jobs in nursing are expected to increase by 25.6 percent. However, according to the National Association of School Nurses, even though school enrollments are projected to increase, school nurse positions are being eliminated in a greater proportion than other positions within the educational system as educational systems try to find ways to cut costs. Since cuts may vary by region and state, school nurses should be flexible and willing to relocate or to seek other nursing opportunities, if necessary.

FOR MORE INFORMATION

For information on careers and training, contact
American Association of Colleges of Nursing
One Dupont Circle, NW, Suite 530
Washington, DC 20036
Tel: 202-463-6930
http://www.aacn.nche.edu

For information on careers and training, and certification, contact the following organizations:

National Association of School Nurses
1416 Park Street, Suite A
Castle Rock, CO 80109
Tel: 303-663-2329
Email: nasn@nasn.org
http://www.nasn.org

For information on certification, contact

National Board for Certification of School Nurses
c/o National Association of School Nurses
1416 Park Street, Suite A
Castle Rock, CO 80109
303-663-2329
certification@nbcsn.com
http://www.nbcsn.com

INTERVIEW

Betsy Gidley is a school nurse in Greenville, North Carolina. She was kind enough to discuss her career with the editors of Careers in Focus: Child Care.

Q. How long have you been a school nurse? Where do you work?

A. I have been a school nurse for nine years. I work at Pitt County Memorial Hospital. Although I'm employed by the hospital, I serve students in the Pitt County schools. I am assigned two elementary schools at present.

Q. Why did you decide to become a school nurse?

A. After receiving my B.S. degree in education, I was an elementary school teacher for about six years. I then received my Master's degree in library science and was a media coordinator for about 11 years. I received my B.S. degree in nursing from East Carolina University. I began as a critical care nurse and then became a rehab nurse. As a single parent, the shifts were difficult, so I decided to try school nursing. It has been a perfect mix of nursing in an educational setting.

Q. What are your typical tasks/responsibilities as a school nurse?

A. Every day in school nursing is different! I case manage students and staff with chronic health conditions (i.e., diabetes, ADHD, asthma, seizure disorders, etc.), as well as triage those with acute health issues. I serve as a health resource for parents, students, and staff who need education on various health problems and provide educational sessions, health fairs, or in-services. I also monitor the medications/medical procedures that teachers give in schools to ensure that they are using proper technique and protocol. Lastly, I assist in screening students for potential vision/dental issues.

Q. **What are the most important professional qualities for school nurses?**

A. The most important qualities for potential school nurses include flexibility, good problem-solving skills, good critical thinking skills, and a broad nursing knowledge base.

Q. **What advice would you give to high school students who are interested in this career?**

A. Students who are interested in a future career in school nursing should volunteer at homeless shelters or on pediatric floors in hospitals, and become members of service organizations. Mentoring younger students or helping in daycare/after school settings is also important. Membership in a health career club or becoming a candy striper would be helpful as well.

Social Workers

OVERVIEW

Social workers help people and communities solve problems. These problems include poverty, racism, discrimination, physical and mental illness, addiction, and abuse. They counsel individuals and families, they lead group sessions, they research social problems, and they develop policy and programs. Social workers are dedicated to empowering people and helping people to preserve their dignity and worth. Approximately 477,000 social workers are employed in the United States; 274,000 of this group are child, family, and school social workers.

HISTORY

Even before the United States became a country, poverty and unemployment were among society's problems. Almshouses and shelters that provided the homeless with jobs and rooms were established as early as 1657. The social work profession as we know it today, however, has its origins in the "friendly visitor" of the early 1800s. These charity workers went from home to home offering guidance in how to move beyond the troubles of poverty.

At a time when not much financial assistance was available from local governments, the poor relied on friendly visitors for instruction on household budgeting and educating their children. Despite their good intentions, however, the friendly visitors could not provide the poor with all the necessary support. The middle-class women who served as friendly visitors were generally far removed from the experiences of the lower classes. Most of the friendly visitors served the community for only a very short time and therefore did not have the opportunity to gain much experience with the poor. The great difference between the life experiences of the friendly visitors and the experiences of their clients sometimes resulted in serious problems: The self-esteem and ambitions of the poor were sometimes damaged by the moral judgments of the friendly visitors. In some cases, friendly visitors only promoted their middle-class values and practices.

By the late 1800s, many charitable organizations developed in U.S. and Canadian cities. With the development of these organizations came a deeper insight into improving the conditions of the poor. Serving as a friendly visitor came to be considered an apprenticeship; it became necessary for friendly visitors to build better relationships with their clients. Friendly visitors were encouraged to take the time to learn about their clients and to develop an understanding of each client's individual needs. Nevertheless, some sense of moral superiority remained, as these charitable organizations refused assistance to alcoholics, beggars, and prostitutes.

The birth of the settlement house brought charity workers even closer to their clients. Settlement houses served as communities for the poor and were staffed by young, well-educated idealists anxious to solve society's problems. The staff people lived among their clients and learned from them. In 1889, Jane Addams established the best known of the settlement houses, a community in Chicago called Hull House. Addams wrote extensively of the problems of the poor, and her efforts to provide solutions led to the foundation of social work education. She emphasized the importance of an education specific to the concerns of the social worker. By the 1920s, social work master's degree programs were established in many universities.

Theories and methodologies of social work have changed over the years, but the basis of the profession has remained the same: helping people and addressing social problems. As society changes, so do its problems, calling for redefinition of the social work profession. The first three fields of formal social work were defined by setting: medical social work; psychiatric social work; and child welfare. Later, practice was classified by different methodologies: casework; group work; and community organization. Most recently, the social work profession has been divided into two areas—direct practice and indirect practice.

THE JOB

After months of physical abuse from her husband, a young woman has taken her children and moved out of her house. With no job and no home, and fearing for her safety, she looks for a temporary shelter for herself and her children. Once there, she can rely on the help of social workers who will provide her with a room, food, and security. The social workers will offer counseling and emotional support to help her address the problems in her life. They will involve her in group sessions with other victims of abuse. They will direct her to job-training programs and other employment services. They will set up interviews with managers of low-income housing. As the woman makes efforts to improve her life, the shelter will provide day care for the children. All these resources exist because the social work profession has long been committed to empowering people and improving society.

The social worker's role extends even beyond the shelter. If the woman has trouble getting help from other agencies, the social worker will serve as an advocate, stepping in to ensure that she gets the aid to which she is entitled. The woman may also qualify for long-term assistance from the shelter, such as a second-step program in which a social worker offers counseling and other support over several months. The woman's individual experience will also help in the social worker's research of the problem of domestic violence; with that research, the social worker can help the community come to a better understanding of the problem and can direct society toward solutions. Some of these solutions may include the development of special police procedures for domestic disputes, or court-ordered therapy groups for abusive spouses.

Direct social work practice is also known as clinical practice. As the name suggests, direct practice involves working directly with the client by offering counseling, advocacy, information and referral, and education. Indirect practice concerns the structures through which the direct practice is offered. Indirect practice (a practice consisting mostly of social workers with Ph.D.'s) involves program development and evaluation, administration, and policy analysis. The vast majority of the more than 153,000 members of the National Association of Social Workers (NASW) work in direct service roles.

Because of the number of problems facing individuals, families and communities, social workers find jobs in a variety of settings and with a variety of client groups. Some of these areas are discussed in the following paragraphs.

Health/mental health care. Mental health care has become the lead area of social work employment. These jobs are competitive and typically go to more experienced social workers. Settings include community mental health centers, where social workers serve persistently mentally ill people and participate in outreach services; state and county mental hospitals, for long-term, inpatient care; facilities of the

Department of Veterans Affairs, involving a variety of mental health care programs for veterans; and private psychiatric hospitals, for patients who can pay directly. Social workers also work with patients who have physical illnesses. They help individuals and their families adjust to the illness and the changes that illness may bring to their lives. They confer with physicians and with other members of the medical team to make plans about the best way to help the patient. They explain the treatment and its anticipated outcome to both the patient and the family. They help the patient adjust to the possible prospect of long hospitalization and isolation from the family.

Child care/family services. Efforts are being made to offer a more universal system of care that would incorporate child care, family services, and community service. Child care services include day care homes, child care centers, and Head Start centers. Social workers in this setting attempt to address all the problems children face from infancy to late adolescence. They work with families to detect problems early and intervene when necessary. They research the problems confronting children and families, and they establish new services or adapt existing services to address these problems. They provide parenting education to teenage parents, which can involve living with a teenage mother in a foster care situation, teaching parenting skills, and caring for the baby while the mother attends school. Social workers alert employers to employees' needs for daytime child care.

Social workers in this area of service are constantly required to address new issues; in recent years, for example, social workers have developed services for families composed of different cultural backgrounds, services for children with congenital disabilities resulting from the mother's drug use, and disabilities related to HIV or AIDS.

Geriatric social work. Within this field, social workers provide individual and family counseling services in order to assess the older person's needs and strengths. Social workers help older people locate transportation and housing services. They also offer adult day care services, or adult foster care services that match older people with families. Adult protective services protect older people from abuse and neglect, and respite services allow family members time off from the care of an older person. A little-recognized problem is the rising incidence of AIDS among the elderly; 10 percent of all AIDS patients are aged 50 or over.

School social work. In schools, social workers serve students and their families, teachers, administrators, and other school staff members. Education, counseling, and advocacy are important aspects of school social work. With education, social workers attempt to prevent alcohol and drug abuse, teen pregnancy, and the spread of

AIDS and other sexually transmitted diseases. They provide multi-cultural and family life education. They counsel students who are discriminated against because of their sexual orientation or racial, ethnic, or religious background. They also serve as advocates for these students, bringing issues of discrimination before administrators, school boards, and student councils.

A smaller number of social workers are employed in the areas of social work education (a field composed of the professors and instructors who teach and train students of social work); group practice (in which social workers facilitate treatment and support groups); and corrections (providing services to inmates in penal institutions). Social workers also offer counseling, occupational assistance, and advocacy to those with addictions and disabilities, to the homeless, and to women, children, and the elderly who have been in abusive situations.

Client groups expand and change as societal problems change. Social work professionals must remain aware of the problems affecting individuals and communities in order to offer assistance to as many people as possible.

Computers have become important tools for social workers. Client records are maintained on computers, allowing for easier collection and analysis of data. Interactive computer programs are used in training social workers, as well as to analyze case histories (such as for an individual's risk of HIV infection).

REQUIREMENTS

High School

To prepare for social work, you should take courses in high school that will improve your communications skills, such as English, speech, and composition. On a debate team, you could further develop your skills in communication as well as research and analysis. History, social studies, and sociology courses are important in understanding the concerns and issues of society. Although some work is available for those with only a high school diploma or associate degree (as a social work aide or social services technician), the most opportunities exist for people with degrees in social work.

Postsecondary Training

There are approximately 436 B.S.W. (bachelor's in social work) programs and 149 M.S.W. (master's in social work) programs accredited by the Council on Social Work Education. The Group for the Advancement of Doctoral Education lists 78 doctoral programs for

Ph.D. programs in social work or D.S.W. (doctor of social work) programs. The Council on Social Work Education requires that five areas be covered in accredited bachelor's degree social work programs: human behavior and the social environment; social welfare policy and services; social work practice; research; and field practicum. Most programs require two years of liberal arts study followed by two years of study in the social work major. Also, students must complete a field practicum of at least 400 hours. Graduates of these programs can find work in public assistance or they can work with the elderly or with people with mental or developmental disabilities.

Although no clear lines of classification are drawn in the social work profession, most supervisory and administrative positions require at least an M.S.W. degree. Master's programs are organized according to fields of practice (such as mental health care), problem areas (substance abuse), population groups (the elderly), and practice roles (practice with individuals, families, or communities). They are usually two-year programs that require at least 900 hours of field practice. Most positions in mental health care facilities require an M.S.W. Doctoral degrees are also available and prepare students for research and teaching. Most social workers with doctorates go to work in community organizations.

Certification or Licensing

Licensing, certification, or registration of social workers is required by all states. To receive the necessary licensing, a social worker will typically have to gain a certain amount of experience and also pass an exam. Five voluntary certification programs help to identify those social workers who have gained the knowledge and experience necessary to meet national standards.

The National Association of Social Workers offers voluntary credentials to social workers with an M.S.W. degree, based on their experience: the academy of certified social workers (ACSW), the qualified clinical social worker (QCSW), or the diplomate in clinical social work (DCSW). These credentials are particularly valuable for social workers in private practice, as some health insurance providers require them for reimbursement purposes.

Other Requirements

Social work requires great dedication. As a social worker, you have the responsibility of helping whole families, groups, and communities, as well as focusing on the needs of individuals. Your efforts will not always be supported by the society at large; sometimes you must work against a community's prejudice, disinterest, and denial. You

Did You Know?

- The first social work class was offered in 1898 at Columbia University in New York.

- Social work is one of the fastest growing careers in the United States. Employment is expected to grow by 30 percent by 2010.

- Social workers are the largest group of mental health services providers in the United States.

- Politicians with a background in social work include Senator Barbara Mikulski (D-Md.), Senator Debbie Stabenow (D-Mich.), Representative Barbara Lee (D-Calif.), Representative Edolphus Towns (D-N.Y.), and Representative Susan Davis (D-Calif.).

Sources: U.S. Department of Labor, Substance Abuse and Mental Health Services Administration, National Association of Social Workers

must also remain sensitive to the problems of your clients, offering support, and not moral judgment or personal bias. The only way to effectively address new social problems and new client groups is to remain open to the thoughts and needs of all human beings. Assessing situations and solving problems requires clarity of vision and a genuine concern for the well-being of others.

With this clarity of vision, your work will be all the more rewarding. Social workers have the satisfaction of making a connection with other people and helping them through difficult times. Along with the rewards, however, the work can provide a great deal of stress. Hearing repeatedly about the deeply troubled lives of prison inmates, the mentally ill, abused women and children, and others can be depressing and defeating. Trying to convince society of the need for changes in laws and services can be a long, hard struggle. You must have perseverance to fight for your clients against all odds.

EXPLORING

As a high school student, you may find openings for summer or part-time work as a receptionist or file clerk with a local social service agency. If there is no opportunity for paid employment, you could work as a volunteer. You can also gain good experience by working as a counselor in a camp for children with physical, mental, or developmental disabilities. Your local YMCA, park district, or other recreational facility may need volunteers for group recreation programs, including programs designed for the prevention of delinquency. By reporting for your high school newspaper, you'll have the opportunity to interview people, conduct surveys, and research social change, all of which are important aspects of the social work profession.

You could also volunteer a few afternoons a week to read to people in retirement homes or to the blind. Work as a tutor in special education programs is sometimes available to high school students.

EMPLOYERS

Social workers can be employed in direct or clinical practice, providing individual and family counseling services, or they may work as administrators for the organizations that provide direct practice. Social workers are employed by community health and mental health centers; hospitals and mental hospitals; child care, family services, and community service organizations, including day care and Head Start programs; elderly care programs, including adult protective services and adult day care and foster care; prisons; shelters and halfway houses; schools; courts; and nursing homes.

STARTING OUT

Most students of social work pursue a master's degree and in the process learn about the variety of jobs available. They also make valuable connections through faculty and other students. Through the university's career services office or an internship program, a student will learn about job openings and potential employers.

A social work education in an accredited program will provide you with the most opportunities, and the best salaries and chances for promotion, but practical social work experience can also earn you full-time employment. A part-time job or volunteer work will introduce you to social work professionals who can provide you with career guidance and letters of reference. Agencies with limited funding may not be able to afford to hire social workers with M.S.W.'s and will therefore look for applicants with a great deal of experience and lower salary expectations.

ADVANCEMENT

The attractive and better paying jobs tend to go to those with more years of practical experience. Dedication to your job, an extensive resume, and good references will lead to advancement in the profession. Also, many social work programs offer continuing education workshops, courses, and seminars. These refresher courses help practicing social workers to refine their skills and to learn about new areas of practice and new methods and problems. The courses are intended to supplement your social work education, not substitute for a bachelor's or master's degree. These continuing education courses can lead to job promotions and salary increases.

EARNINGS

The more education a social worker has completed, the more money he or she stands to make in the profession. The area of practice also determines earnings; the areas of mental health, group services, and community organization and planning provide higher salaries, while elderly and disabled care generally provide lower pay. Salaries also vary among regions. Social workers on the east and west coasts earn higher salaries than those in the Midwest. During their first five years of practice, social workers' salaries generally increase faster than in later years.

The median salary range for child, family, and school social workers was $35,010 in 2004, according to the U.S. Department of Labor. The top 10 percent earned more than $58,410, while the lowest 10 percent earned less than $23,470. Medical and public health social workers' salaries ranged from less than $23,840 to more than $56,320 in 2002, according to the *Occupational Outlook Handbook,* and mental health and substance abuse workers earned between $21,050 and $52,240.

WORK ENVIRONMENT

Social workers do not always work at a desk. When they do, they may be interviewing clients, writing reports, or conferring with other staff members. Depending on the size of the agency, office duties such as typing letters, filing, and answering phones may be performed by an aide or volunteer. Social workers employed at shelters or halfway houses may spend most of their time with clients, tutoring, counseling, or leading groups.

Some social workers have to drive to remote areas to make a home visit. They may go into inner city neighborhoods, schools, courts, or jails. In larger cities, domestic violence and homeless shelters are sometimes located in rundown or dangerous areas. Most social workers are involved directly with the people they serve and must carefully examine the client's living conditions and family relations. Although some of these living conditions can be pleasant and demonstrate a good home situation, others can be squalid and depressing.

Advocacy involves work in a variety of different environments. Although much of this work may require making phone calls and sending faxes and letters, it also requires meetings with clients' employers, directors of agencies, local legislators, and others. It may sometimes require testifying in court as well.

OUTLOOK

The field of social work is expected to grow faster than the average for all other occupations through 2012, according to the U.S. Department of Labor. The greatest factor for this growth is the increased number of older people who are in need of social services. Social workers who specialize in gerontology will find many job opportunities in nursing homes, hospitals, and home health care agencies. The needs of the future elderly population are likely to be different from those of the present elderly. Currently, the elderly appreciate community living, while subsequent generations may demand more individual care.

Schools will also need more social workers to deal with issues such as teenage pregnancies, children from single-parent households, and any adjustment problems recent immigrants may have. The trend to integrate students with disabilities into the general school population will require the expertise of social workers to make the transition smoother. However, job availability in schools will depend on funding given by state and local sources.

To help control costs, hospitals are encouraging early discharge for some of their patients. Social workers will be needed by hospitals to help secure health services for patients in their homes. There is also a growing number of people with physical disabilities or impairments staying in their own homes, requiring home health care workers.

Increased availability of health insurance funding and the growing number of people able to pay for professional help will create opportunities for those in private practice. Many businesses hire social workers to help in employee assistance programs, often on a contractual basis.

Poverty is still a main issue that social workers address. Families are finding it increasingly challenging to make ends meet on wages that are just barely above the minimum. The problem of fathers who do not make their court-ordered child support payments forces single mothers to work more than one job or rely on welfare. An increased awareness of domestic violence has also pointed up the fact that many of the homeless and unemployed are women who have left abusive situations. Besides all this, working with the poor is often considered unattractive, leaving many social work positions in this area unfilled.

Competition for jobs in urban areas will remain strong. However, there is still a shortage of social workers in rural areas; these areas usually cannot offer the high salaries or modern facilities that attract large numbers of applicants.

The social work profession is constantly changing. The survival of social service agencies, both private and public, depends on shifting political, economic, and workplace issues.

Social work professionals are worried about the threat of declassification. Because of budget constraints and a need for more workers, some agencies have lowered their job requirements. When unable to afford qualified professionals, they hire those with less education and experience. This downgrading raises questions about quality of care and professional standards. Just as in some situations low salaries push out the qualified social worker, so do high salaries. In the area of corrections, attractive salaries (up to $40,000 for someone with a two-year associate degree) have resulted in more competition from other service workers.

Liability is another growing concern. If a social worker, for example, tries to prove that a child has been beaten or attempts to remove a child from his or her home, the worker can potentially be sued for libel. At the other extreme, a social worker can face criminal charges for failure to remove a child from an abusive home. More social workers are taking out malpractice insurance.

FOR MORE INFORMATION

For information on social work careers and accredited educational programs, contact
Council on Social Work Education
1725 Duke Street, Suite 500
Alexandria, VA 22314-3457
Tel: 703-683-8080
Email: info@cswe.org
http://www.cswe.org

To access the online publication Choices: Careers in Social Work, *contact*
National Association of Social Workers
750 First Street, NE, Suite 700
Washington, DC 20002-4241

Tel: 202-408-8600
Email: info@naswdc.org
http://www.naswdc.org

For information on educational programs in Canada, contact
Canadian Association of Schools of Social Work
1398 Star Top Road
Ottawa, ON K1B 4V7
Canada
Tel: 613-792-1953
Email: cassw@cassw-acess.ca
http://www.cassw-acess.ca

Special Education Teachers

OVERVIEW

Special education teachers teach students ages three to 21 who have a variety of disabilities. They design individualized education plans and work with students one-on-one to help them learn academic subjects and life skills. Approximately 433,000 special education teachers are employed in the United States, mostly in public schools.

HISTORY

Modern special education traces its origins to 16th-century Spain, where Pedro Ponce de Leon and Juan Pablo Bonet taught deaf students to read and write. It was not until the late 18th century that education for the blind was initiated. An early example was an institute for blind children in Paris that was founded by Valentin Huay. The first U.S. schools for the blind were founded in 1832 in Boston and New York.

By the early 19th century, attempts were made to educate the mentally handicapped. Edouard Sequin, a French psychiatrist, established the first school for the mentally handicapped in 1939 in Orange, New Jersey.

In the first half of the 20th century, special education became increasingly popular in the United States. By the 1960s and early 1970s, parents began to lobby state and local officials for improved special education programs for their children with disabilities. To address continuing inequities in the public education of special needs students, Congress passed the Education for All Handicapped Children Act (Public Law 94-142) in 1975. The act required public schools to provide disabled students with a "free appropriate education" in the "least restrictive environment" possible. The act was reauthorized in 1990, 1997, and 2004, and renamed the Individuals with Disabilities Education Act. This act allows approximately 7 million children to receive special education services from highly trained special education teachers.

THE JOB

Special education teachers instruct students who have a variety of disabilities. Their students may have physical disabilities, such as vision, hearing, or orthopedic impairment. They may also have learning disabilities or serious emotional disturbances. Although less common, special education teachers sometimes work with students who are gifted and talented, children who have limited proficiency in English, children who have communicable diseases, or children who are neglected and abused.

In order to teach special education students, these teachers design and modify instruction so that it is tailored to individual student needs. Teachers collaborate with school psychologists, social workers, parents, and occupational, physical, and speech-language therapists to develop a specially designed Individualized Education Program (IEP) for each of their students. The IEP sets personalized goals for a student based upon his or her learning style and ability, and it outlines specific steps to prepare him or her for employment or postsecondary schooling.

Special education teachers teach at a pace that is dictated by the individual needs and abilities of their students. Unlike most regular classes, special education classes do not have an established curriculum that is taught to all students at the same time. Because student abilities vary widely, instruction is individualized; it is part of the teacher's responsibility to match specific techniques with a student's learning style and abilities. They may spend much time working with students one-on-one or in small groups.

Working with different types of students requires a variety of teaching methods. Some students may need to use special equipment or skills in the classroom in order to overcome their disabilities. For example, a teacher working with a student with a physical disability might use a computer that is operated by touching a screen or by voice commands. To work with hearing-impaired students, the teacher may need to use sign language. With visually impaired students, he or she may use teaching materials that have Braille characters or large, easy-to-see type. Gifted and talented students may

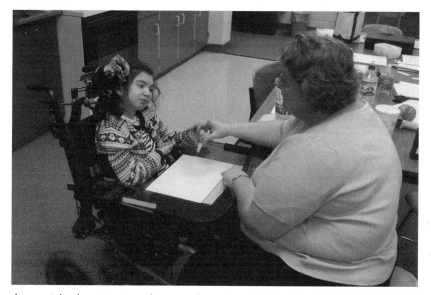

A special education teacher works with a child with physical disabilities. *(Jim Whitmer Photography)*

need extra challenging assignments, a faster learning pace, or special attention in one curriculum area, such as art or music.

In addition to teaching academic subjects, special education teachers help students develop both emotionally and socially. They work to make students as independent as possible by teaching them functional skills for daily living. They may help young children learn basic grooming, hygiene, and table manners. Older students might be taught how to balance a checkbook, follow a recipe, or use the public transportation system.

Special education teachers meet regularly with their students' parents to inform them of their child's progress and offer suggestions of how to promote learning at home. They may also meet with school administrators, social workers, psychologists, various types of therapists, and students' general education teachers.

The current trend in education is to integrate students with disabilities into regular classrooms to the extent that it is possible and beneficial to them. This is often called "mainstreaming." As mainstreaming becomes increasingly common, special education teachers frequently work with general education teachers in general education classrooms. They may help adapt curriculum materials and teaching techniques to meet the needs of students with disabilities and offer guidance on dealing with students' emotional and behavioral problems.

In addition to working with students, special education teachers are responsible for a certain amount of paperwork. They document each student's progress and may fill out any forms that are required by the school system or the government.

REQUIREMENTS
High School
If you are considering a career as a special education teacher, you should focus on courses that will prepare you for college. These classes include natural and social sciences, mathematics, and English. Speech classes would also be a good choice for improving your communication skills. Finally, classes in psychology might be helpful both to help you understand the students you will eventually teach, and prepare you for college-level psychology course work.

Postsecondary Training
All states require that teachers have at least a bachelor's degree and that they complete a prescribed number of subject and education credits. It is increasingly common for special education teachers to complete an additional fifth year of training after they receive their bachelor's degree. Many states require special education teachers to get a master's degree in special education.

There are approximately 800 colleges and universities in the United States that offer programs in special education, including undergraduate, master's, and doctoral programs. These programs include general and specialized courses in special education, including educational psychology, legal issues of special education, child growth and development, and knowledge and skills needed for teaching students with disabilities. The student typically spends the last year of the program student teaching in an actual classroom, under the supervision of a licensed teacher.

Certification or Licensing
All states require that special education teachers be licensed, although the particulars of licensing vary by state. In some states, these teachers must first be certified as elementary or secondary school teachers and then meet specific requirements to teach special education. Some states offer general special education licensure; others license several different subspecialties within special education. Some states allow special education teachers to transfer their license from one state to another, but many still require these teachers to pass licensing requirements for that state.

Other Requirements

To be successful in this field, you need to have many of the same personal characteristics as other classroom teachers: the ability to communicate, a broad knowledge of the arts, sciences, and history, and a love of children. In addition, you will need a great deal of patience and persistence. You need to be creative, flexible, cooperative, and accepting of differences in others. Finally, you need to be emotionally stable and consistent in your dealings with students.

EXPLORING

There are a number of ways to explore the field of special education. One of the first and easiest is to approach a special education teacher at his or her school and ask to talk about the job. Perhaps the teacher could provide a tour of the special education classroom or allow you to visit while a class is in session.

You might also want to become acquainted with special-needs students at your own school or become involved in a school or community mentoring program for these students. There may also be other opportunities for volunteer work or part-time jobs in schools, community agencies, camps, or residential facilities that will allow you to work with persons with disabilities.

EMPLOYERS

The majority of special education teachers teach in public and private schools. Others work in state education agencies, homebound or hospital environments, or residential facilities.

STARTING OUT

Because public school systems are by far the largest employers of special education teachers, this is where you should begin your job search.

You can also use your college's career placement center to locate job leads. This may prove a very effective place to begin. You may also write to your state's department of education for information on placement and regulations, or contact state employment offices to inquire about job openings. Applying directly to local school systems can sometimes be effective. Even if a school system does not have an immediate opening, it will usually keep your resume on file should a vacancy occur.

ADVANCEMENT

Advancement opportunities for special education teachers, as for regular classroom teachers, are fairly limited. They may take the form of higher wages, better facilities, or more prestige. In some cases, these teachers advance to become supervisors or administrators, although this may require continued education on the teacher's part. Another option is for special education teachers to earn advanced degrees and become instructors at the college level.

EARNINGS

In some school districts, salaries for special education teachers follow the same scale as general education teachers. In 2004, the median annual salary for special education teachers working in preschools, kindergartens, and elementary schools was $44,330, according to the U.S. Department of Labor. Special education teachers working in middle schools had median annual earnings of $45,000, and those in secondary schools earned $46,300. The lowest paid 10 percent of all special education teachers made less than $30,410 a year, and the highest paid 10 percent made more than $75,390. Private school teachers usually earn less than their public school counterparts. Teachers can supplement their annual salaries by becoming an activity sponsor, or by summer work. Some school districts pay their special education teachers on a separate scale, which is usually higher than that of general education teachers.

In 2002, almost 62 percent of all special education teachers belonged to unions, which help them secure fair working hours, salaries, and working conditions.

Regardless of the salary scale, special education teachers usually receive a complete benefits package, which includes health and life insurance, paid holidays and vacations, and a pension plan.

WORK ENVIRONMENT

Special education teachers usually work from 7:30 or 8:00 A.M. to 3:00 or 3:30 P.M. Like most teachers, however, they typically spend several hours in the evening grading papers, completing paperwork, or preparing lessons for the next day. Altogether, most special education teachers work more than the standard 40 hours per week.

Although some schools offer year-round classes for students, the majority of special education teachers work the traditional 10-month school year, with a two-month vacation in the summer. Many teachers find this work schedule very appealing, as it gives them the opportunity to pursue personal interests or additional education during the summer break. Teachers typically also get a week off at Christmas and for spring break.

Special education teachers work in a variety of settings in schools, including both ordinary and specially equipped classrooms, resource rooms, and therapy rooms. Some schools have newer and better facilities for special education than others. Although it is less common, some teachers work in residential facilities or tutor students who are homebound or hospitalized.

Working with special education students can be very demanding, due to their physical and emotional needs. Teachers may fight a constant battle to keep certain students, particularly those with behavior disorders, under control. Other students, such as those with mental impairments or learning disabilities, learn so slowly that it may seem as if they are making no progress. The special education teacher must deal daily with frustration, setbacks, and classroom disturbances.

These teachers must also contend with heavy workloads, including a great deal of paperwork to document each student's progress. In addition, they may sometimes be faced with irate parents who feel that their child is not receiving proper treatment or an adequate education.

The positive side of this job is that special education teachers help students overcome their disabilities and learn to be as functional as possible. For a special education teacher, knowing that he or she is making a difference in a child's life can be very rewarding and emotionally fulfilling.

OUTLOOK

The field of special education is expected to grow faster than the average through 2012, according to the U.S. Department of Labor. This demand is caused partly by the growth in the number of special education students needing services. Medical advances resulting in more survivors of illness and accidents, a rise in birth defects, increased awareness and understanding of learning disabilities, and general population growth are also significant factors for strong demand. Because of the rise in the number of youths with disabilities under the age of 21, the government has given approval for more federally funded programs. Growth of jobs in this field has also been influenced positively by legislation emphasizing training and employment for individuals with disabilities and a growing public awareness and interest in those with disabilities.

Finally, there is a fairly high turnover rate in this field, as special education teachers find the work too stressful and switch to mainstream teaching or change jobs altogether. Many job openings will arise out of a need to replace teachers who leave their positions. There is a shortage of qualified teachers in rural areas and in the inner city. Jobs will also be plentiful for teachers who specialize in speech and language impairments, learning disabilities, and early childhood intervention. Bilingual teachers with multicultural experience will be in high demand.

FOR MORE INFORMATION

For information on current issues, legal cases, and conferences, contact
   Council of Administrators of Special Education
   Fort Valley State University
   1005 State University Drive
   Fort Valley, GA 31030
   Tel: 418-825-7667
   http://www.casecec.org

For links to more information on special education, visit
   SPED Online
   http://www.spedonline.com

Speech-Language Pathologists and Audiologists

OVERVIEW

Speech-language pathologists and *audiologists* help people who have speech and hearing defects. They identify the problem and use tests to further evaluate it. Speech-language pathologists try to improve the speech and language skills of clients with communications disorders. Audiologists perform tests to measure the hearing ability of clients who may range in age from the very young to the very old. Since it is not uncommon for clients to require both speech and hearing assistance, pathologists and audiologists may frequently work together to help clients. Some professionals decide to combine these jobs into one, working as *speech-language pathologists/audiologists*. Audiologists and speech-language pathologists may work for school systems, in private practice, and at clinics and other medical facilities. Other employment possibilities for these professionals are teaching at colleges and universities and conducting research on what causes certain speech and hearing defects. There are approximately 105,000 speech-language pathologists and audiologists employed in the United States.

HISTORY

The diagnosis and treatment of speech and hearing defects is a new part of medical science. In the past, physicians weren't able to help patients with these types of problems because there was usually nothing visibly wrong, and little was known about how speech and hearing were related. Until the middle of the 19th century, medical researchers did not know whether speech defects were caused by lack of hearing, or whether the patient was the victim of two separate ailments. And even if they could figure out why something was wrong, doctors still could not communicate with the patient.

Alexander Graham Bell, the inventor of the telephone, provided some of the answers. His grandfather taught elocution (the art of public speaking), and Bell grew up interested in the problems of speech and hearing. It became his profession, and by 1871 Bell was lecturing to a class of teachers of deaf people at Boston University. Soon afterward, Bell opened his own school, where he experimented with the idea of making speech visible to his pupils. If he could make them see the movements made by different human tones, they could speak by learning to produce similar vibrations. Bell's efforts not only helped deaf people of his day, but also led directly to the invention of the telephone in 1876. Probably the most famous deaf person was Helen Keller, whose teacher, Anne Sullivan, applied the discoveries of Bell to help Keller overcome her blindness and deafness.

THE JOB

Even though the two professions seem to blend together at times, speech-language pathology and audiology are very different from one another. However, because both speech and hearing are related to one another, a person competent in one discipline must have familiarity with the other.

The duties performed by speech-language pathologists and audiologists differ depending on education and experience and place of employment. Most speech-language pathologists provide direct clinical services to individuals and independently develop and carry out treatment programs. In medical facilities, they may work with physicians, social workers, psychologists, and other therapists to develop and execute treatment plans. In a school environment, they develop individual or group programs, counsel parents, and sometimes help teachers with classroom activities.

Clients of speech-language pathologists include people who cannot make speech sounds, or cannot make them clearly; those with speech rhythm and fluency problems such as stuttering; people with voice quality problems, such as inappropriate pitch or harsh voice; those with problems understanding and producing language; and those with cognitive communication impairments, such as attention, memory, and problem-solving disorders. Speech-language pathologists may also work with people who have oral motor problems that cause eating and swallowing difficulties. Clients' problems may be congenital, developmental, or acquired and caused by hearing loss, brain injury or deterioration, cerebral palsy, stroke, cleft palate, voice pathology, mental retardation, or emotional problems.

Speech-language pathologists conduct written and oral tests and use special instruments to analyze and diagnose the nature and extent of impairment. They develop an individualized plan of care, which may include automated devices and sign language. They teach clients how to make sounds, improve their voices, or increase their language skills to communicate more effectively. Speech-language pathologists help clients develop, or recover, reliable communication skills.

People who have hearing, balance, and related problems consult audiologists, who use audiometers and other testing devices to discover the nature and extent of hearing loss. Audiologists interpret these results and may coordinate them with medical, educational, and psychological information to make a diagnosis and determine a course of treatment.

Hearing disorders can result from trauma at birth, viral infections, genetic disorders, or exposure to loud noise. Treatment may include examining and cleaning the ear canal, fitting and dispensing a hearing aid or other device, and audiologic rehabilitation (including auditory training or instruction in speech or lip reading). Audiologists provide fitting and tuning of cochlear implants and help those with implants adjust to the implant amplification systems. They also test noise levels in workplaces and conduct hearing protection programs in industry, as well as in schools and communities.

Audiologists provide direct clinical services to clients and sometimes develop and implement individual treatment programs. In some environments, however, they work as members of professional teams in planning and implementing treatment plans.

In a research environment, speech-language pathologists and audiologists investigate communicative disorders and their causes and ways to improve clinical services. Those teaching in colleges and universities instruct students on the principles and bases of communication, communication disorders, and clinical techniques used in speech and hearing.

Speech-language pathologists and audiologists keep records on the initial evaluation, progress, and discharge of clients to identify problems and track progress. They counsel individuals and their families on how to cope with the stress and misunderstanding that often accompany communication disorders.

REQUIREMENTS

High School

Since a college degree is a must for practicing this profession, make sure your high school classes are geared toward preparing you for higher education. Health and science classes, including biology, are very important. Mathematics classes and English classes will help you develop the math, research, and writing skills you will need in college. Because speech-language pathologists and audiologists work so intensely with language, you may also find it beneficial to study a foreign language, paying special attention to how you learn to make sounds and remember words. Speech classes will also improve your awareness of sounds and language as well as improve your speaking and listening skills.

Postsecondary Training

Most states require a master's degree in speech-language pathology or audiology for a beginning job in either profession. Typical majors for those going into this field include communication sciences and disorders, speech and hearing, or education. Regardless of your career goal (speech-language pathologist or audiologist), your undergraduate course work should include classes in anatomy, biology, physiology, physics, and other related areas, such as linguistics, semantics, and phonetics. It is also helpful to have some exposure to child psychology.

To be eligible for certification, which most employers and states require, you must have at least a master's degree from a program accredited by the accreditation council of the American Speech-Language-Hearing Association (ASHA). According to the ASHA, as of 2012, audiologists will have to earn a doctorate in order to be certified. Currently there are more than 400 programs in speech-language pathology and/or audiology; however, not all of these programs are accredited. It is in your best interest to contact ASHA for a listing of accredited programs before you decide on a graduate school to attend. Some schools offer graduate degrees only in speech-language pathology or graduate degrees only in audiology. A number of schools offer degrees in both fields. Graduate-level course work in audiology includes such studies as hearing and language disorders, normal auditory and speech-language development, balance, and audiology instrumentation. Graduate-level work for those in speech-language pathology includes studies in evaluating and treating speech and language disorders, stuttering, pronunciation, and voice modulation. Students of both disciplines are required to complete supervised clinical fieldwork or practicum.

If you plan to go into research, teaching, or administration, you will need to complete a doctorate degree.

Certification or Licensing

To work as a speech pathologist or audiologist in a public school, you will be required to be a certified teacher, and you must meet special state requirements if treating children with disabilities. Almost all states regulate audiology and/or speech-language pathology through licensure or title registration, and all but a handful require continuing education for license renewal. In order to become licensed, you must have completed an advanced degree in the field (generally a master's degree, but a doctorate is becoming the new standard for audiologists), pass a standardized test, and complete 300 to 375 hours of supervised clinical experience and nine months of postgraduate professional clinical experience. Some states permit audiologists to dispense hearing aids under an audiology license. Specific education and experience requirements, type of regulation, and title use vary by state.

Many states base their licensing laws on ASHA certification. ASHA offers speech-language pathologists the certificate of clinical competence in speech-language pathology and audiologists the certificate of clinical competence in audiology. To be eligible for these certifications, you must meet certain education requirements, such as the supervised clinical fieldwork experience, and have completed a postgraduate clinical fellowship. The fellowship must be no less than 36 weeks of full-time professional employment or its part-time equivalent. You must then pass an examination in the area in which you want certification.

Other Requirements

Naturally, speech-language pathologists and audiologists should have strong communication skills. Note, though, that this means more than being able to speak clearly. You must be able to explain diagnostic test results and treatment plans in an easily understood way for a variety of clients who are already experiencing problems. As a speech-language pathologist and audiologist, you should enjoy working with people, both your clients and other professionals who may be involved in the client's treatment. In addition, you need patience and compassion. A client's progress may be slow, and you should be supportive and encouraging during these times.

EXPLORING

Although the specialized nature of this work makes it difficult for you to get an informal introduction to either profession, there are opportunities to be found. Official training must begin at the college or university level, but it is possible for you to volunteer in clinics and hospitals. As a prospective speech-language pathologist and audiologist, you may also find it helpful to learn sign language or volunteer your time in speech, language, and hearing centers.

EMPLOYERS

According to the *Occupational Outlook Handbook,* there are about 105,000 speech-language pathologists and audiologists employed in the United States. About one-half of speech-language pathologists are employed in education, from elementary school to the university level. More than half of audiologists work in physicians' offices and medical facilities. Other professionals in this field work in state and local governments, hearing aid stores, and scientific research facilities. A small but growing number of speech-language pathologists and audiologists are in private practice, generally working with patients referred to them by physicians and other health practitioners.

Some speech-language pathologists and audiologists contract to provide services in schools, hospitals, or nursing homes, or work as consultants to industry.

STARTING OUT

If you want to work in the public school systems, your college career services office can help you with interviewing skills. Professors sometimes know of job openings and may even post these openings on a centrally located bulletin board. It may be possible to find employment by contacting a hospital or rehabilitation center. To work in colleges and universities as a specialist in the classroom, clinic, or research center, it is almost mandatory to be working on a graduate degree. Many scholarships, fellowships, and grants for assistants are available in colleges and universities giving courses in speech-language pathology and audiology. Most of these and other assistance programs are offered at the graduate level. The U.S. Rehabilitation

Services Administration, the Children's Bureau, the U.S. Department of Education, and the National Institutes of Health allocate funds for teaching and training grants to colleges and universities with graduate study programs. In addition, the Department of Veterans Affairs provides stipends (a fixed allowance) for predoctoral work.

ADVANCEMENT

Advancement in speech-language pathology and audiology is based chiefly on education. Individuals who have completed graduate study will have the best opportunities to enter research and administrative areas, supervising other speech-language pathologists or audiologists either in developmental work or in public school systems.

EARNINGS

In 2004, speech-language pathologists earned a median annual salary of $53,790, according to the U.S. Department of Labor. Salaries ranged from to less than $35,820 to more than $84,310. Also in 2004, audiologists earned a median annual salary of $53,040. The lowest 10 percent of these workers earned less than $36,500, while the highest 10 percent earned $80,190 or more per year. Geographic location and type of facility are important salary variables. Almost all employment situations provide fringe benefits such as paid vacations, sick leave, and retirement programs.

WORK ENVIRONMENT

Most speech-language pathologists and audiologists work 40 hours a week at a desk or table in clean comfortable surroundings. Speech-language pathologists and audiologists who focus on research, however, may work longer hours. The job is not physically demanding but does require attention to detail and intense concentration. The emotional needs of clients and their families may be demanding.

OUTLOOK

Population growth, lengthening life spans, and increased public awareness of the problems associated with communicative disorders indicate a highly favorable employment outlook for well-qualified personnel. The U.S. Department of Labor predicts that employment for speech-language pathologists and audiologists will grow faster than the average through 2012. Much of this growth depends on economic factors, further budget cutbacks by health care providers and third-party payers, and legal mandates requiring services for people with disabilities.

Nearly half of the new jobs emerging through the end of the decade are expected to be in speech and hearing clinics, physicians' offices, and outpatient care facilities. Speech-language pathologists and audiologists will be needed in these places, for example, to carry out the increasing number of rehabilitation programs for stroke victims and patients with head injuries.

Substantial job growth will continue to occur in elementary and secondary schools because of the Individuals with Disabilities Education Act. The law guarantees special education and related services to minors with disabilities.

Many new jobs will be created in hospitals, nursing homes, rehabilitation centers, and home health agencies; most of these openings will probably be filled by private practitioners employed on a contract basis. Opportunities for speech-language pathologists and audiologists in private practice should increase in the future. There should be a greater demand for consultant audiologists in the area of industrial and environmental noise as manufacturing and other companies develop and carry out noise-control programs.

FOR MORE INFORMATION

The American Auditory Society is concerned with hearing disorders, how to prevent them, and the rehabilitation of individuals with hearing and balance dysfunction.
American Auditory Society
352 Sundial Ridge Circle
Dammeron Valley, UT 84783
Tel: 435-574-0062
http://www.amauditorysoc.org

This professional, scientific, and credentialing association offers information about communication disorders and career and membership information.
American Speech-Language-Hearing Association
10801 Rockville Pike
Rockville, MD 20852
Tel: 800-638-8255
Email: actioncenter@asha.org
http://www.asha.org

This association is for undergraduate and graduate students study-ing human communication. For news related to the field and to find out about regional chapters, contact

National Student Speech, Language, and Hearing Association
10801 Rockville Pike
Rockville, MD 20852
Tel: 800-498-2071
Email: nsslha@asha.org
http://www.nsslha.org

Teacher Aides

OVERVIEW

Teacher aides perform a wide variety of duties to help teachers run a classroom. Teacher aides prepare instructional materials, help students with classroom work, and supervise students in the library, on the playground, and at lunch. They perform administrative duties such as photocopying, keeping attendance records, and grading papers. There are approximately 1.3 million teacher aides employed in the United States.

HISTORY

As formal education became more widely available in the 20th century, teachers' jobs became more complex. The size of classes increased, and a growing educational bureaucracy demanded that more records be kept of students' achievements and classroom activities. Advancements in technology, changes in educational theory, and a great increase in the amount and variety of teaching materials all contributed to the time required to prepare materials and assess student progress, leaving teachers less time for the teaching for which they had been trained.

To remedy this problem, teacher aides began to be employed to take care of the more routine aspects of running an instructional program. Today, many schools and school districts employ teacher aides, to the great benefit of hardworking teachers and students.

THE JOB

Teacher aides work in public, private, and parochial preschools and elementary and secondary schools. Their duties vary depending on the classroom teacher, school, and school district. Some teacher aides specialize in one subject, and some work in a specific type of school setting. These settings include bilingual classrooms, gifted and talented programs, classes for learning disabled students and those with unique physical needs, and multi-age classrooms. These aides conduct the same type of classroom work as other teacher aides, but they may provide more individual assistance to students.

Fran Moker works as a teacher aide in a dropout prevention unit of a middle school. Her work involves enrolling students in the unit and explaining the program to parents. She maintains files on the students and attends to other administrative duties. "I work directly with the sixth, seventh, and eighth grade teachers," Moker says, "making all the copies, setting up conferences, and grading papers. I also cover their classes when necessary for short periods of time to give the teachers a break." She also works directly with students, tutoring and advising. "I listen to students when they have problems," she says. "We work with at-risk students, so it's necessary to be supportive. Many of our students come from broken homes and have parents with serious drug and alcohol problems. Consistent caring is a must."

No matter what kind of classroom they assist in, teacher aides will likely copy, compile, and hand out class materials, set up and operate audiovisual equipment, arrange field trips, and type or word-process materials. They organize classroom files, including grade reports, attendance, and health records. They may also obtain library materials and order classroom supplies.

Teacher aides may be in charge of keeping order in classrooms, school cafeterias, libraries, hallways, and playgrounds. Often, they wait with preschool and elementary students coming to or leaving school and make sure all students are accounted for. When a class leaves its room for such subjects as art, music, physical education, or computer lab, teacher aides may go with the students to help the teachers of these other subjects.

Another responsibility of teacher aides is correcting and grading homework and tests, usually for objective assignments and tests that require specific answers. They use answer sheets to mark students' papers and examinations and keep records of students' scores. In some large schools, an aide may be called a *grading clerk* and be responsible only for scoring objective tests and computing and recording test scores. Often using an electronic grading machine or computer, the grading clerk totals errors found and computes the percentage of questions answered correctly. The clerk then records this score and averages students' test scores to determine their grade for the course.

Earnings by Industry

Industry	Employment	Mean Annual Earnings
Elementary and secondary schools	997,460	$20,710
Child day care services	95,940	$17,790
Colleges and universities	39,210	$25,060
Junior colleges	19,050	$24,710
Individual and family services	15,500	$19,450

Source: U.S. Department of Labor, 2004

Under the teacher's supervision, teacher aides may work directly with students in the classroom. They listen to a group of young students read aloud or involve the class in a special project such as a science fair, art project, or drama production. With older students, teacher aides provide review or study sessions prior to exams or give extra help with research projects or homework. Some teacher aides work with individual students in a tutorial setting, helping in areas of special need or concern. They may work with the teacher to prepare lesson plans, bibliographies, charts, or maps. They may help to decorate the classroom, design bulletin boards and displays, and arrange workstations. Teacher aides may also participate in parent-teacher conferences to discuss students' progress.

REQUIREMENTS

High School

Courses in English, history, social studies, mathematics, art, drama, physical education, and the sciences will provide you with a broad base of knowledge. This knowledge will enable you to help students learn in these same subjects. Knowledge of a second language can be an asset, especially when working in schools with bilingual student, parent, or staff populations. Courses in child care, home economics, and psychology are also valuable for this career. You should try to gain some experience working with computers; students at many elementary schools and even preschools now do a large amount of computer work, and computer skills are important in performing clerical duties.

Postsecondary Training

Postsecondary requirements for teacher aides depend on the school or school district and the kinds of responsibilities the aides have. In districts where aides perform mostly clerical duties, applicants may need only to have a high school diploma or the equivalent, a general equivalency diploma (GED). Those who work in the classroom may be required to take some college courses and attend in-service training and special teacher conferences and seminars. The No Child Left Behind Act of 2001 created even more stringent educational requirements for teacher assistants employed in Title 1 schools—those that have a large proportion of students from low-income households. Teacher assistants in these schools must meet one of three requirements: have at least two years of college, have a two-year degree or higher, or pass a state and local assessment. Previous experience working with children, a valid driver's license, and the passing of a background check may be also required for assistants employed in Title 1 schools. Some schools and districts may help you pay some of the costs involved in attending these programs. Often community and junior colleges have certificate and associate degree programs that prepare teacher aides for classroom work, offering courses in child development, health and safety, and child guidance.

Newly hired aides participate in orientation sessions and formal training at the school. In these sessions, aides learn about the school's organization, operation, and philosophy. They learn how to keep school records, operate audiovisual equipment, check books out of the library, and administer first aid.

Many schools prefer to hire teacher aides who have some experience working with children; some schools prefer to hire workers who live within the school district. Schools may also require that you pass written exams and health physicals. You must be able to work effectively with both children and adults and should have good verbal and written communication skills.

Other Requirements

You must enjoy working with children and be able to handle their demands, problems, and questions with patience and fairness. You must be willing and able to follow instructions, but also should be able to take the initiative in projects. Flexibility, creativity, and a cheerful outlook are definite assets for anyone working with children. You should find out the specific job requirements from the school, school district, or state department of education in the area where you would like to work. Requirements vary from school to school and state to state. It is important to remember that an aide who is qualified to work in one state, or even one school, may not be qualified to work in another.

EXPLORING

You can gain experience working with children by volunteering to help with religious education classes at your place of worship. You may volunteer to help with scouting troops or work as a counselor at a summer camp. You may have the opportunity to volunteer to help coach a children's athletic team or work with children in after-school programs at community centers. Babysitting is a common way to gain experience in working with children and to learn about the different stages of child development.

EMPLOYERS

Approximately 1.3 million workers are employed as teacher assistants in the United States. About 40 percent of teacher assistants work part time. With the national shortage of teachers, aides can find work in just about any preschool, elementary, or secondary school in the country. Teacher aides also assist in special education programs and in group home settings. Aides work in both public and private schools.

STARTING OUT

You can apply directly to schools and school districts for teacher aide positions. Many school districts and state departments of education maintain job listings, bulletin boards, and hotlines that list available job openings. Teacher aide jobs are often advertised in the classified section of the newspaper. Once you are hired as a teacher aide, you will spend the first months in special training and will receive a beginning wage. After six months or so, you'll have regular responsibilities and possibly a wage increase.

ADVANCEMENT

Teacher aides usually advance only in terms of increases in salary or responsibility, which come with experience. Aides in some districts may receive time off to take college courses. Some teacher aides choose to pursue bachelor's degrees and fulfill the licensing requirements of the state or school to become teachers. "I will probably always remain in the education field," Fran Moker says, "maybe someday returning to school to get a degree in education."

Some aides, who find that they enjoy the administrative side of the job, may move into school or district office staff positions. Others choose to get more training and then work as resource teachers, tutors, guidance counselors, or reading, mathematics, or speech specialists. Some teacher aides go into school library work or become media specialists. While it is true that most of these jobs require additional training, the job of teacher aide is a good place to begin.

EARNINGS

Teacher aides are usually paid on an hourly basis and usually only during the nine or 10 months of the school calendar. Salaries vary depending on the school or district, region of the country, and the duties the aides perform. Median annual earnings of teacher assistants were $19,760 in 2004, according to the U.S. Department of Labor. Salaries ranged from less than $13,150 to more than $29,850.

Benefits such as health insurance and vacation or sick leave may also depend on the school or district as well as the number of hours a teacher aide works. Many schools employ teacher aides only part time and do not offer such benefits. Other teacher aides may receive the same health and pension benefits as the teachers in their school and be covered under collective bargaining agreements.

WORK ENVIRONMENT

Teacher aides work in a well-lit, comfortable, wheelchair-accessible environment, although some older school buildings may be in disrepair with unpredictable heating or cooling systems. Most of their work will be indoors, but teacher aides will spend some time outside before and after school, and during recess and lunch hours, to watch over the students. They are often on their feet, monitoring the halls and lunch areas and running errands for teachers. Although this work is not physically strenuous, working closely with children can be stressful and tiring.

Teacher aides find it rewarding to help students learn and develop. The pay, however, is not as rewarding. "As with all those in the entire education field," Fran Moker says, "we are grossly underpaid. But that's the only negative. I truly enjoy my job." Because of her commitment to her work, Fran is allowed certain benefits, such as time off when needed.

OUTLOOK

Growth in this field is expected to be somewhat faster than the average through 2012 because of an expected increase in school enrollments, but especially the student population that requires assistance of teacher aides, including special education students and students for whom English is not their first language. As the number of students in schools increases, new schools and classrooms will be added, and more teachers and teacher aides will be hired. A shortage of teachers will cause administrators to hire more aides to help with larger classrooms. Because of increased responsibilities for aides, state departments of education will likely establish standards of training. The National Resource Center for Paraprofessionals is designing national standards for paraeducator training.

The No Child Left Behind Act will also increase demand for teacher aides, due to a greater focus on educational quality and accountability. Teachers will need aides to help students prepare for standardized testing and assist those students who perform poorly on standardized tests.

The field of special education (working with students with specific learning, emotional, or physical concerns or disabilities) is expected to grow rapidly, and more aides will be needed in these areas. The Individuals with Disabilities Education Act requires a more specialized training for aides working with students with disabilities. Teacher aides who want to work with young children in day care or extended day programs will have a relatively easy time finding work because more children are attending these programs while their parents are at work.

FOR MORE INFORMATION

To learn about current issues affecting paraprofessionals in education, visit the AFT website or contact
   American Federation of Teachers (AFT)
   555 New Jersey Avenue, NW
   Washington, DC 20001
   Tel: 202-879-4400
   Email: online@aft.org
   http://www.aft.org

To order publications or read current research and other information, contact

Association for Childhood Education International
17904 Georgia Avenue, Suite 215
Olney, MD 20832
Tel: 800-423-3563
Email: headquarters@acei.org
http://www.acei.org

For information about training programs and other resources, contact

National Resource Center for Paraprofessionals
Utah State University
6526 Old Main Hill
Logan, UT 84322-6526
Tel: 435-797-7272
Email: info@nrcpara.org
http://www.nrcpara.org

Index

Entries and page numbers in **bold** indicate major treatment of a topic.

D